Before Object, After Image
Koshirakura Landscape 1996–2006

Before Object, After Image:
Koshirakura Landscape 1996–2006
Shin Egashira

Editor Pamela Johnston
Design Nadine Rinderer

Before Object, After Image accompanies an exhibition
held at the Architectural Association from 6 October to
1 November 2006. It has been produced through the
AA Print Studio with the support of Allon Kaye, David
Terrien and Clare Barrett.

AA Publications are initiated by the Director of the
AA School, Brett Steele.

Printed in England by Dexter Graphics

ISBN 978-1-902902-55-5

AA Publications
36 Bedford Square
London WC1B 3ES
Telephone + 44 (0)20 7887 4021
Fax + 44 (0)20 7414 0783

publications@aaschool.ac.uk
aaschool.ac.uk/publications

Contents

This book brings together the drawings, photographs, diaries and memories of a remarkable decade-long series of summer workshops led by the architect Shin Egashira in the remote village of Koshirakura in northern Japan. In many respects the carefully crafted structures and small built interventions produced by the workshop stand apart from much contemporary architectural thinking (including its teaching and its production). They also evade the clichés that fatally intertwine contemporary architecture and its globalisation.

What we see here is a kind of inverse order of World City and Distant Village, directly connecting Shin's London-based teaching with the experiences of a tiny village in the mountains north of Tokyo (which Shin notes in his epilogue is directly under the flight path of his annual journeys from Heathrow to Tokyo's Narita airport). The modest but highly refined projects blend the local and the global in a way that is ultimately the most convincing part of the entire enterprise, bringing together young students from around the world with an ageing local population that is gradually being cut off from the surrounding region and economy.

The small timber and stone structures that have evolved over the duration of this workshop are most important for being the outcome of collective effort and experience – between students, teacher and the local community. What matters more than plain architectural description is the way in which the life of the village itself has been renovated and rejuvenated by the sustained, regular addition of a group of young students from abroad.

One of the least remarked-on features of contemporary architectural thinking is that of time. Too often, architectural projects consist of fast, 'one off' interventions intended to create something 'new' atop an already existing site or condition. It's a before/after syndrome typical of much of contemporary cultural production. Of the countless beautiful features of the architectural sensibility of Shin and his students, the most immediately apparent, and important, is that of duration. Here we see architectural thinking surrendered over to an understanding of gradual processes of change. We witness this in the most obvious way, by seeing a project unfold, literally, over many years, in successive cycles and iterative project interventions. Some of the structures are planned one year (during the construction of an entirely different project); others are reworked a year or two after their initial completion.

Given the underlying presence of time as the dominant architectural force influencing the results of the workshop, I am reminded of the artist Robert Smithson and his essays on the role of time in land art. Smithson was also fascinated with the real presence of time in built projects, which he observed in the gradual ways that any building site, even the most conventional, undergoes constant change throughout its life. Steve Reich wrote as a contemporary of Smithson in the 1970s about the ways in which in his music compositions could be seen to be a 'gradual process' of subtle change and adjustment which, while nearly indiscernible, nonetheless gives overall form and structure.

We can see a similar, highly refined attention to form as the outcome of gradual processes, in the remarkable cumulative effect of the workshop series documented in this book, where we observe an architecture shaped by, and giving form to, the passage of time.

There are many to thank for this beautiful book: first and foremost, the more than 200 students whose design inventions, manual labour and extended energies literally gave shape to every aspect of the annual projects in the village. Equally (and any good teacher is never more than equal to his or her students) I would like to thank Shin Egashira, not only for his incredible vision, commitment and belief, which have driven the whole project, but also for having shared so much of this work over the past years at the Architectural Association. Thanks to the many participants in the workshop for their diaries, essays and texts, which have helped to bring the projects to life. We are grateful for the kind support of many individuals and organisations, whose financial and material assistance has made the workshops possible. I would like in particular to thank the Maeda Corporation for their generous support of the book, which we are pleased to publish on the occasion of the exhibition 'Before Object, After Image' shown at the AA. Collectively, what we are all able to enjoy here is an architecture of immense optimism, beauty and individuality. Enjoy.

Brett Steele
Director, AA School
London, October 2006

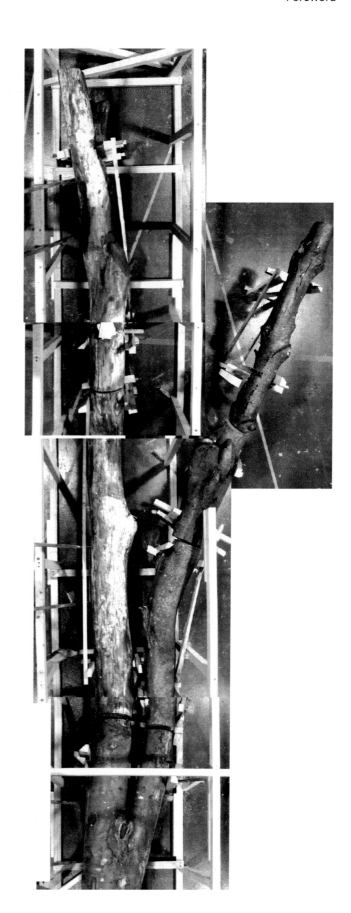

Above: A plan view of seven beech trunks, jig and six cuts, Hooke Park, Dorset 2006.
The idea for the 'Before Object, After Image' exhibition at the AA was to initiate a tree-cutting festival specific to Bedford Square – a parallel to the Maple Tree festival that is specific to Koshirakura. It was hoped that a maple tree could be brought from Japan. Practicality necessitated looking closer to home. Though no maples could be found in Hooke Park, beech trees abound. The cuts in the tree seen here were dictated by a geometry taken from the Koshirakura landscape, and the mapping of the co-ordinates of projects built over the workshop's 10 years. The seven sections of tree set off on their journey to the AA Gallery equipped with legs on wheels. Each section of the tree houses a projector displaying images from the workshops (see following spread).

Size, Scale and Distance

If the dimensions of objects were the size of the space they occupy in our mind, we would perhaps see file sizes appearing after images of objects and events. We would be able to sort all the images ever seen with our eyes and compress or rearrange them into non-linear orders – 'pop', 'stack' and 'push' – just as PowerBooks manage our memories externally. We could animate them into different sequences, zooming in and out, and project them onto a screen as large as we wished.

As current technologies continue to develop as extensions of our individual senses, we are becoming more familiar with recursive systems, where one thing will often emerge simultaneously as details of many. We are learning not to assume that there are coherent rules ensuring that details are part of a larger configuration, that stories belong to their context, or that objects are smaller than the landscape. Thus when we make objects in the landscape, there might be a landscape represented within the details of the objects. It's like the world of Lewis Carroll where Alice simultaneously gets bigger and smaller as she moves through the looking glass, where there are sizes within a size, scales within a scale. Even a simple question such as 'Is 1:1000 scale bigger or smaller than 1:1?' can become quite confusing. This could have been a question to Alice before she went through the looking glass.

Six-year-olds sitting an elementary school entrance exam in Japan are asked another question:
'*What will become larger when objects shrink smaller?*'
Answer:
'*The number of wrinkles.*'
'*Age*'...
An architectural answer might be:
'*The gaps between objects.*'
In relation to the Koshirakura Workshop we might ask:
'*How long is 10 years?...*'
(Or 12 months of summer sessions spread over a decade, to be precise.)

'*And what has been achieved?*'
Answer:
'*Perhaps nothing of significance, in the context of the history inscribed upon the complex topography of Koshirakura by snow and water, or the number of graceful wrinkles etched by laughter on the faces of the villagers over a long period of time.*'

As we enter the landscape of Koshirakura, our sense of scale is naturally challenged by the child-size furniture that surrounds us in the old elementary school where we stay. The prevailing atmosphere helps us to feel rather comfortably lost in a time that can be described as a combination of rest and activity.

The workshop began with very clear intentions. The rejuvenation of post-agricultural communities in rural Japan seemed to be a challenging agenda for new forms of architectural fieldwork that would not be possible in a studio-based, academic environment. Our intentions were soon diverted, however, by the discovery of a fascinating sense of autonomy in the place, as well as by romantic notions of being in a remote village. We were even more seduced by the inherent sense of beauty we found there – the directness of life-expressions, which made architectural formalities seem insignificant, combined with the strange contrast between the place (agricultural and rural) and us (international and urban).

Contrast provided a way to reinterpret things that were familiar to the locals, or to communicate differences. Thus our initial workshop began by documenting what we could see and how we saw ourselves in the details of their scenery. It was an attempt to combine the processes of design and documentation. We made maps and found ways to position our bodies in the landscape by making chairs, documenting the landscape by turning it into forms of communication.

Our report to the government after the first workshop consisted of photographs of the

'Before Object, After Image' installation in AA Gallery, October 2006.

community and our group making objects and maps, and drinking and working together for one of their festivals. It was not what they had expected. They had thought we would submit a list of design suggestions to improve the village and sketch-plans to illustrate ways of reusing existing facilities.

Luckily the government was perceptive at this stage and changed the purpose of the workshop from design survey to communication programme, to allow funding to continue.

What is design?

In his book *Architectural Model as Machine* Albert C Smith suggests, 'The architectural-scale model machine is one of the mechanisms humans create to measure and test their various concepts of the invisible … The architectural model is a thinking mechanism used in making the invisible visible.'

We use objects of various scales to help us learn to recognise the architecture of space before and after building: 3d models, physical models, mock-ups, diagrams, maquettes. It is through these models that we recognise structures that might otherwise be too big, too small, too close, too far away, too fast or too slow to be seen all at once. Models demonstrate combined sets of relationships by bringing things together across distances. Perhaps it is a set of scales and rules that makes the models architecture.

During the workshop in Koshirakura, there is no distance between site and studio, models and site; no difference between local people and the people who represent locals. The meaning of representation changes in face of the ambiguity between designing and making.

We often make models on site and draw full-scale diagrams on the ground. We look at photographs and video footage of the context within the context. We make detail components and then discover possible scales by comparing them to other things. We find the right size by repeating inherent patterns of the detail as we enlarge and shrink its proportions.

Perhaps the language gap opens up creative opportunities for communication and interpretation as making models became our first language. When the model evolves at the place, and is anchored to the pile foundations, we may still see it as a model on site, at a 1:1 scale. And the question is always, 'What is this building a model of?', or 'What does this model represent?'

For instance, in the construction of the Bus Shelter we did not want to determine the built form at the outset. Each team made a series of details that spoke about its experience of the landscape of Koshirakura. When these textural models were pieced together they began to find their scale in relation to each other, to form lines for reading the landscape they were originally borrowed from. Once we brought them into being, we could see the structure as a collection of detail samples that spoke about the landscape. So how can we say that we made the Bus Shelter?

– Let's put a few details together and see what they become.
– And repeat this several times to see if there is any moment at which this collection of things begins to have a particular pattern.
– Let's draw a map of the unmapped and see what could not have been mapped with it.
– And see if we can borrow geometry from the village and rearrange details with it.
– How far can we push this process?
– The result will be a continuous project, which never seems to end. Models will become models of others.
– Every time we arrange details, different scales emerge.
– Relocating models within the context suggests different sizes.
– Seen from inside and outside the model, the landscape seems to shrink and expand.
– Things get bigger and smaller simultaneously.
– Climatic forces seem to require everything to be in a state of incompletion: stand on the site on a high summer's day and imagine the whole

place submerged by snow, imagine the absent mass and forces.
– We make full-scale models, details about permeability, angles of slippage and enclosure.
– And then come back the following summer and see if they have worked, by looking at the snow marks left on the sidings.

This kind of detailed approach can help us to suspend our judgements and avoid a fixed vision. It is in fact a very messy process, but it seems to be the right method for productive teamwork. If the same mistake is repeated more than three times, then it is no longer considered a mistake. If it's repeated ten times, it becomes accepted as a ritual or perhaps a habit.

Faced with a lack of facilities, we learned to adapt anything available into a tool and ended up mixing various contrasting senses of distance, time, gravity, textural density and modes of communication.

In 2004 we made a film, 'Real Fiction', by reinventing our constructions as props and stages. Our working methods included on-site filming, making new props, writing filmscripts, acting and editing clips on our laptops, while at the same time searching for good sandstone for foundations, mixing concrete, making timber details with saws and chisels and filming the construction process and inserting it into the main film. We stretched ropes to make a screen and made a small shrine to protect an expensive data projector borrowed from the town hall. On the eve of the festival, sitting on the stone steps of the shrine, waiting for our film to begin, we watched the landscape visible through the screen become a silhouette as the sun set behind it and then was gradually overlapped and replaced by our film scenes in electric blue, glowing ever more brightly in the increasing darkness. When the wind blew through the screen of ropes the image vibrated, giving a sense of movement and immediacy.

As the economic gap between the country and the city becomes more evident, as the authorities restructure their organisations to move further away from local areas, the village appears smaller and the distance of 200 kilometres from Tokyo seems to create a greater sense of remoteness, yet the laughter of the villagers only sounds louder and happier.

It is difficult to address directly the scale of matters that seem to be larger than life. But perhaps we can get a sense of the collective through the details. There are so many stories about one detail, and there are so many details that describe this one story of ten years. The details are the projects; some of them are still in progress, some are becoming parts of others, and the mid-Niigata earthquake of 2004 has destroyed a few links.

This publication attempts to reread the village of Koshirakura by redocumenting details of the landscapes we have mapped, of objects we have made, and of individual diaries that extract different stories from one long event. It presents new maps of the maps, new stories within the diaries, and a new object in the form of a network of the objects.

We would like to see what all these details are becoming a model of, and perhaps locate all the details, events and people within the context of this book. We want to see the village from very close and very far, to give individual views of incidents as well as an overview from 9,000 km away in London.

The publication attempts to locate this village in the field beyond its geography, at the scale of the unknown.

Snow in Uonuma

The Uonuma region of Niigata is only 460 m above sea level and close to the coast. In winter, when a prevailing wind blows fine sand from mainland Asia across the sea, the moisture-laden air freezes into big snowflakes the instant it reaches this northern edge of the Japanese alps. The snow is sticky, very wet and heavy. When it falls in Uonuma, it is easily compressed into solid ice. By the end of the winter, it accumulates up to a depth of 5 m. It is this deep snow that often isolates the villages scattered along the mountainside from the rest of Kawanishi.

There are many small agricultural communities in the rural mountainous landscapes of Japan that are increasingly defined by depopulation, overgrown forests and abandoned rice fields. The name Kawanishi no longer appears on maps printed after April 2005, following the town's absorption into the neighbouring city of Toukamachi.

Geography of Kawanishi

Kawanishi means 'west side of the river'. It is the name of a town on the Shibumi River, a tributary of Japan's longest river, the Shinano. Vast rice fields, irrigated by the river, lie to the east. By contrast, the west side of Kawanishi offers a more complicated topography, with the restless meanders of the Shibumi River cutting deep into the narrow mountain valley.

The mountains are formed of layers of sandy clay of different densities. The instability of this clay base, combined with the steepness of the topography and the force of the snow, continuously reshapes the fragile land surface. Each spring, as the snow melts, geotectonic fault lines and folding patterns are revealed.

Cultivation along the Shibumi

Running along the steep valleys are a series of terraced rice fields. Traditionally the cultivation of the land entailed a continuous negotiation with the behaviour of the river and the forces of snow and landslides. The method known as segai is a way of producing a flat piece of land by manipulating the course of the winding river by carving out a bypass for the water through the hills. In another technique, called mabu, small tunnels are carved out by the farmers. Mabu involves constructing an irrigation system, manipulating a small stream of water and forming terraced fields by artificially creating landslides and sedimentation on the sides of the valley.

Koshirakura Population and Location

Koshirakura is one of 13 small villages scattered along these complex terrains. The landscape is marked by winding roads, small tunnels, thatched roofs, apple orchards on steep slopes and terraced rice-fields, many of which are still being restored after the Niigata earthquake of 2004. Koshirakura's population is now less than 80, a third of what it was 25 years ago; the average age is over 60.

Economic Climate – Local

This landscape is affected not only by the forces of nature, but by the economic constraints upon agriculture since the 1970s. As the young have left, many of the villages have simply ceased to exist. Thatched houses that remain unoccupied soon collapse or are flattened by the weight of the winter snow. Terraced rice fields that are left uncultivated eventually become detached from their irrigation systems and slide down the mountain.

Economic Climate – General

In the late 1970s the Niigata-born former prime minister of Japan, Kakuei Tanaka, established the 'Japanese Islands Rebuilding Plan'. One of its major provisions was for the construction of Japan's longest tunnel to carry the bullet train through the Central Alps, a landscape spanning from Tokyo in the south to Niigata in the north. At the time, it dramatically shrank the notion of distance. However, contrary to Tanaka's vision, it also exaggerated the sense of contrast between the lifestyles in the different places.

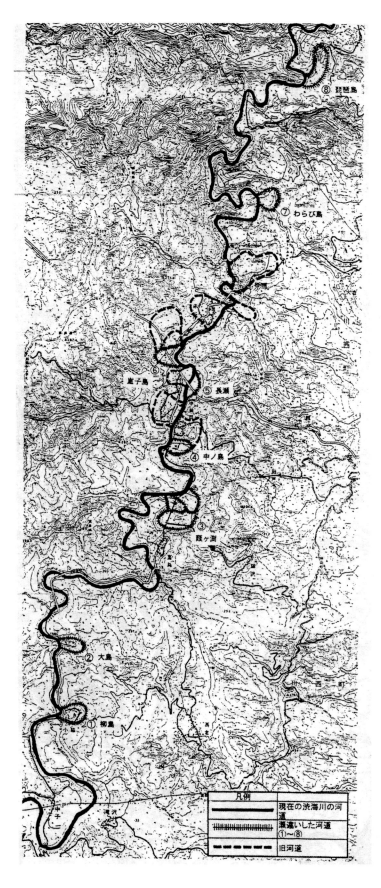

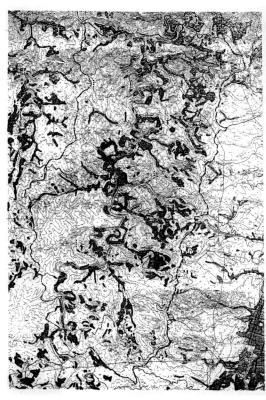

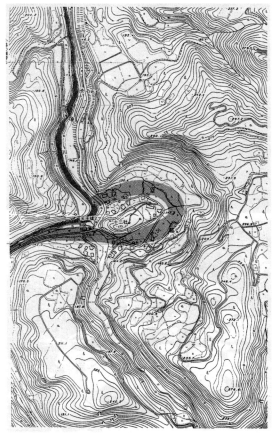

The bullet pipeline encouraged migration from the north to the larger cities in the south; it also promoted a sense of isolation in places like Kawanishi that lay on the path of the speeding train.

Ecomomy – Local Rice/Micro Industries

Kawanishi is also known for Uonuma Koshihikari, the best quality rice in Japan. Although it commands the highest market price, most of the farmers find it difficult to benefit from the trade, partly due to the inherited trading mechanisms of their union, and partly because government legislation encourages them to lower their rice yields to counterbalance increasing rice imports from abroad. Ironically, this was the same government that officially certified Koshirakura as one of the most beautiful 'traditional' rural villages in the country.

Regardless of the economic futility of rice-farming, the community continues to maintain the terraced fields and irrigation systems with the aim of preserving the picturesque views and preventing further landslides. They also continue to produce excellent rice crops on parts of these fields, out of a sense of local pride and for personal pleasure and consumption; other parts of the fields have been converted to provide income from cottage industries such as farming. Most of the residents have two or three jobs which shift seasonally among the family members; grandparents, for instance, often grow rice and carp in the summer and run a small rope-making business in the winter (making, among other things, the ring ropes for sumo wrestling).

Other family-run cottage industries reveal the influence of globalisation. Behind the authentic fabric of these traditional dwellings, with their thatched roofs and modern twists such as integrated satellite dishes, families produce high-precision metal prototype components, supplying companies not only in Japan but also in the USA and Germany.

Snow and Localities

The winter snow, with its weight and volume, is a major force in shaping and reshaping the residents' lifestyles and the buildings of the village. Their daily routines during the winter months include digging out their own houses so as to maintain connections to the main road, and shared duties such as fieldwork and snow clearing. These shared practices extend into seasonal festivities that require a high degree of social cohesion and community participation.

The traditional house, known as *chumon zukuri*, has a steep thatched roof that directs the snow into a pond which is fed by a constant supply of water to prevent it from freezing. The water is drawn from a horizontal well, dug out by hand, that extends several hundred metres into the face of the mountain. In summers past these wells were used as storage.

The pond has always been an important lifeline for the house: it collects melted snow from the roof to prevent the house from collapsing, and the small stream of water that runs along the side of the house clears any snow blocking the path between the street and the entrance. 'Koi' carp are often farmed in the pond, traditionally as a food source during winter, and in the more recent past, when the Nishiki Koi was a popular pet, as a very successful source of income.

Glossary

Gang → enclosed eave
Yokoido → horizontal well
Yukigakoi → snow-shuttering

Opposite, clockwise from left: Map of Shibumi River and its *segai* by-passes; distribution of rice fields; detail of a *segai*.

Changing seasons in Koshirakura.

Above: Early winter. Opposite, clockwise from above:
Early autumn, early summer, early spring.

Below from left to right: Seasonal tools and appliances;
field of Uonoma Koshihikari rice, *chumon zukuri* house.

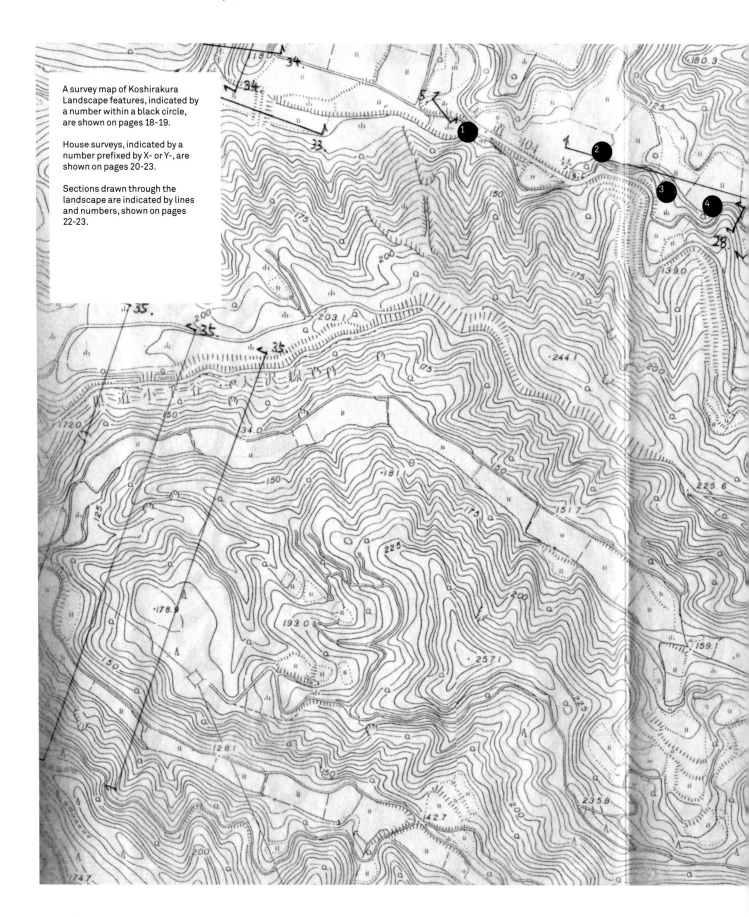

A survey map of Koshirakura
Landscape features, indicated by
a number within a black circle,
are shown on pages 18-19.

House surveys, indicated by a
number prefixed by X- or Y-, are
shown on pages 20-23.

Sections drawn through the
landscape are indicated by lines
and numbers, shown on pages
22-23.

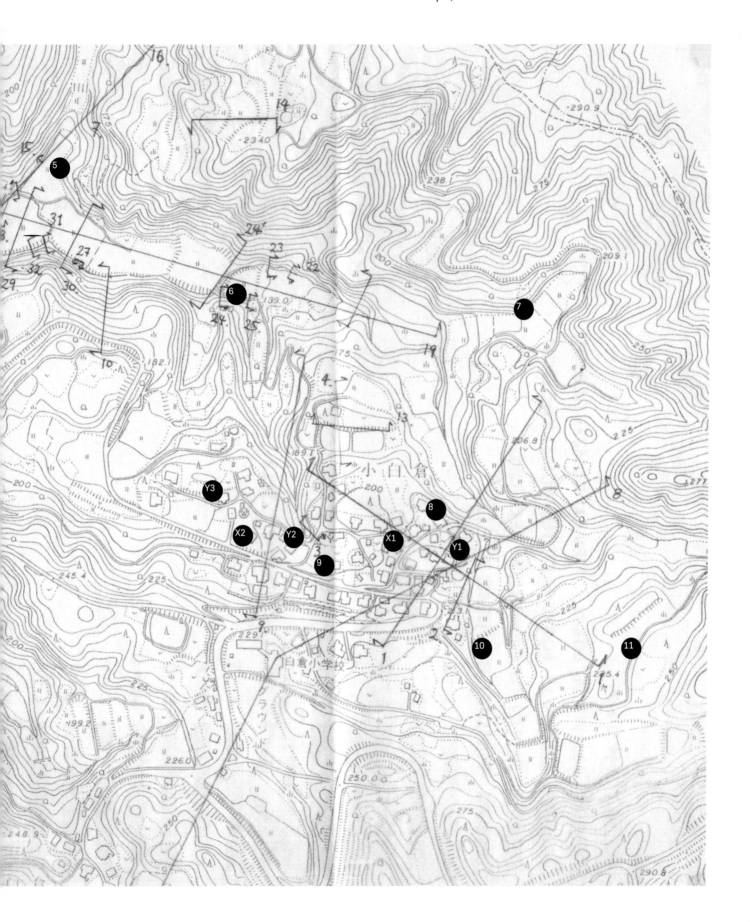

1-2 Exposed strata and folds reveal the geological patterns carved out in the land, a mix of sand and clay in varying proportions.

3-6 *Mabu* in different locations.

7-8 Receding edge of terraced rice field viewed from north edge of village. The upper reaches of the field are overgrown; 9 Carp nursery for communal use; 10 View of rice field from lower edge of village; 11 View of rice field from highest point of village, with converted carp ponds in the foreground.

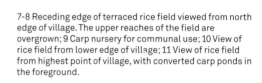

← Second Roof

← Fire protective Shutters

← Snow Barrier

Protective house for Tani-ky Residence   Itani VURA   Y-1

Y-2   Y-3

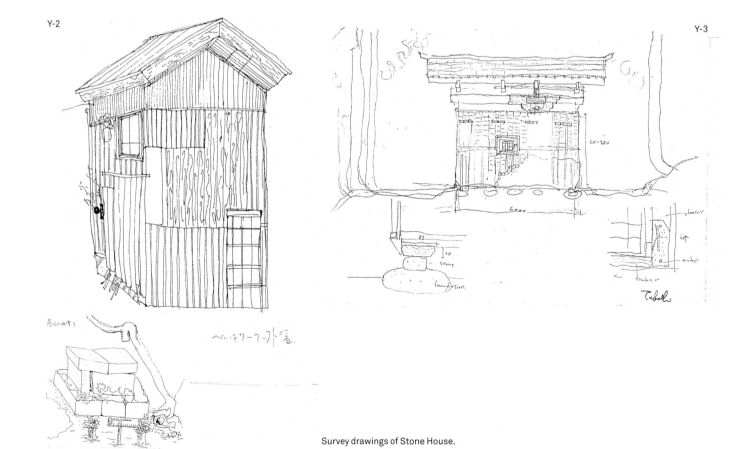

Survey drawings of Stone House.

X-1

X-2

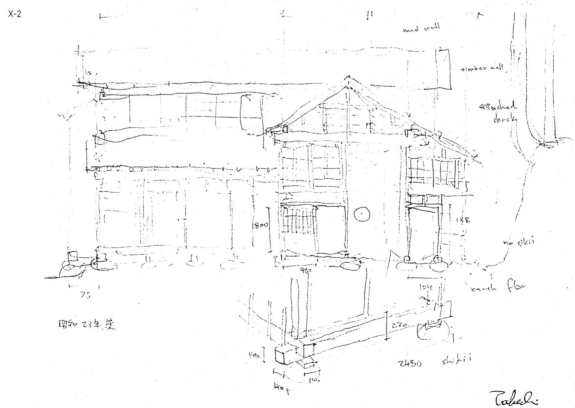

Survey drawings of *chumon zukuri* house.

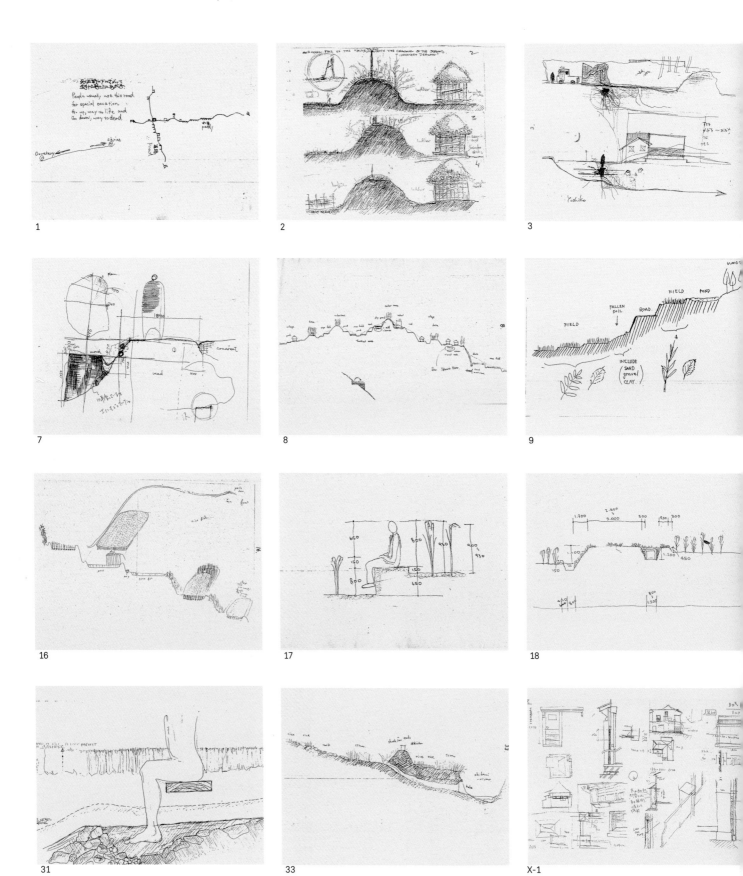

1

2

3

7

8

9

16

17

18

31

33

X-1

5

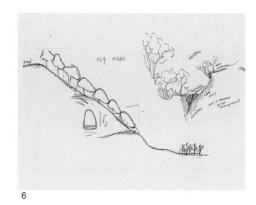

6

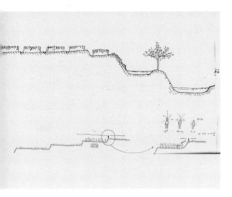

13

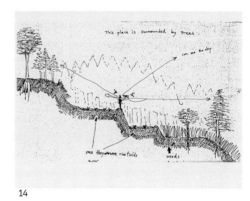

14

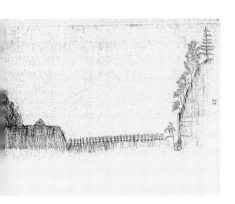

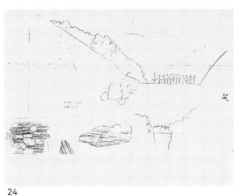

24

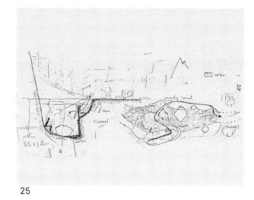

25

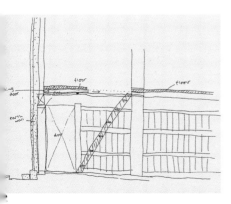

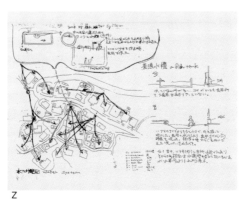

Z

1-33 Sections shown on map on pages 16-17.
X-1 & X-2 Details of *chumon zukuri* house.
Z Network plan of horizontal wells and snow-melting ponds.

From the start, intercultural exchange played an important part in the workshop. The participants needed to be accepted as residents of the village: to achieve this they, in turn, had to accept the duties of residents – cutting grass, learning local songs and supporting the traditional Maple Tree Festival. A tree (which, at this time of year, is inhabited by the god who is being thanked for all blessings) is cut down and carried to the shrine for a night of singing and dancing. The following day it is carried around the village, stopping at houses whose occupants have special reasons to offer thanks to the god and who will consequently provide sake for everyone. The intensity of the festival and the amount of alcohol consumed far exceeded our expectations. In view of the presence of the workshop participants, a larger than usual maple tree was chosen – it visited the school in which the workshop was housed in order to celebrate its continuation.

Chapter 2   Objects and Maps

Kamimura Toryo and Memory Sticks

In the book *Goedel, Escher, Bach* Douglas R Hofstadter discusses how meaning is split between coded message, decoder and receiver. Achilles and the Tortoise try to resolve the question: 'Which contains more information – a record or the phonograph which plays it?'

The tortoise discovers a single record which, when played on different phonographs, produces two different melodies: B_A_C_H and C_A_G_E. It turns out, however, that the two melodies are differentiated only by mechanisms of interval multiplication; in essence they are the same.

Perhaps a similar argument could be applied to drawing and building. Kamimura Toryo, a master carpenter, came to work with us in the summer of 1999 during the construction of the Azumaya (summer pavilion). Toryo does not draw, except on timber. He makes templates when several identical parts are needed. He looked at our drawings and quickly processed all the information in his head; detail components then emerged out of his hands. He could transfer graphics into a set of data.

A simple sketch, indicating only line distances and points, would provide him with enough information to figure out precisely and effortlessly the details and numbers of different components. It was very interesting to see him work alongside Patric Lam, who figured out each detail and dimension using AutoCad.

Toryo also used templates as memory sticks. He looked at our drawings – sections, axos, plans – and asked some questions about details. He made his own diagram – not the drawing we would normally expect, but free-hand lines and points showing the central lines of columns and beams, with some triangul-ations noted either side. This seemed enough for him to estimate most things: amount of materials, working processes, time required to complete the work. While we were using AutoCad to estimate the volume of logs in relation to construction parts, he had already made a mental list of logs to be cut.

Our ambition was to detail everything without using nails and screws. It was our way of paying homage to Toryo and to Japanese carpentry. Toryo looked at our sketch details and asked a few questions, without changing the calm expression on his face. There seemed to be some sort of calculation in progress in his head. 'Can we use steel brackets here and there?', he asked, using one hand as a column and the other held diagonally as a beam, pointing at the junction with his chin. A glance at me, expressionless, to see how I would react to his request. I felt that I was being tested by him. 'It won't be seen from any angle', he added, with a hint of a grin: 'We always do it this way'.

I thought about the misleading image I had built up of Japanese carpentry. My notions were as romanticised as those of foreign admirers of Japanese culture. For instance, I had explained to the students that the thinness of Japanese saws, and their different shapes, are defined by different types of joinery. I had said that each carpenter had his own set of saws which he sharpened every day and never let anyone else touch. Yet the day before we had seen Kamimura Toryo using an electric handheld circular saw to make most of the details.

In fact we were amazed at just how many different ways this cutting machine could be held in one hand against a piece of wood. It somehow reminded me of Jimi Hendrix with his electric guitar held the wrong way around. Toryo was wearing a baseball cap, a sporty pair of sneakers and a T-shirt with a little Snoopy on it – perhaps a Christmas gift from his grandchildren. We liked him a lot.

How it Began: Object in the Landscape

I had been introduced to the Kawanishi Town local government by Mr Ogawa from the Japanese Ministry of Construction, who was working for the prefecture government at the time. He was organising a series of rural regeneration plans that involved introducing architects to rural communities across the moutainous landscape of Niigata.

The government had in fact initiated a variety of different regeneration programmes in this region prior to our workshop. These included promoting academic research (a kind of National Trust), encouraging corporations to set up subsidiaries in the area, selling weekend homes to city-dwellers and creating an alternative holiday resort. None of the programmes had succeeded on account of the remoteness of the place and its harsh climate.

In this context the Town Hall could afford to take a chance on this rather experimental programme which brought a group of international students to the most remote village to see how it worked.

Our unit at the AA had been working on the theme of the object in the landscape, looking at some of the post-industrial landscapes of England (mining regions, derelict areas near nuclear power plants, etc.). Our objective was to recognise the textures of these landscapes as one side of a coin that had the late-twentieth-century construction of the city as its other face. As a result of this experience, we were able to propose a programme in three stages: the reading and repeated rereading of the landscape; the representation of the landscape from details and materials, allowing a reinterpretation of reality from different viewpoints; and the rearranging of these details into new forms of spatial construction.

The workshop had as its base the local elementary school, which had lain empty since it was closed in 1994 due to a shortage of school-age children. Every summer we have replaced the absent children with visiting architectural students.

I have been interested in this project as an observer on the one hand and as a maker on the other. As an observer, I was intrigued to witness the changes taking place in a Japanese rural landscape where traditional means of organising production can no longer be sustained; as an artist I was inspired to document this phenomenon by viewing this landscape as undergoing a process of erasure, in which the ideas of 'place' and 'life-expression' nonetheless retained a sublime essence. At the same time, it was my wish to introduce changes into this landscape by applying architectural knowledge and by making things as means of communication and as forms of direct involvement.

Products of the last 10 years include maps, built artefacts, tools, sections, portraits and films. All of them are linked to each other and informed by a combined sense of the fictional and the actual.

Perhaps the earlier years focused more precisely on aspects of reading and reinventing the natural environment and the existing typology of Koshirakura. Then the workshop gradually shifted towards the construction of physical changes, evident in structures such as the Azumaya and Viewing Platform. In recent years the work has begun to suggest alternative notions of recycling and reusing not only materials and land, but also importantly memories, using film as a means to organise the physical space of temporality.

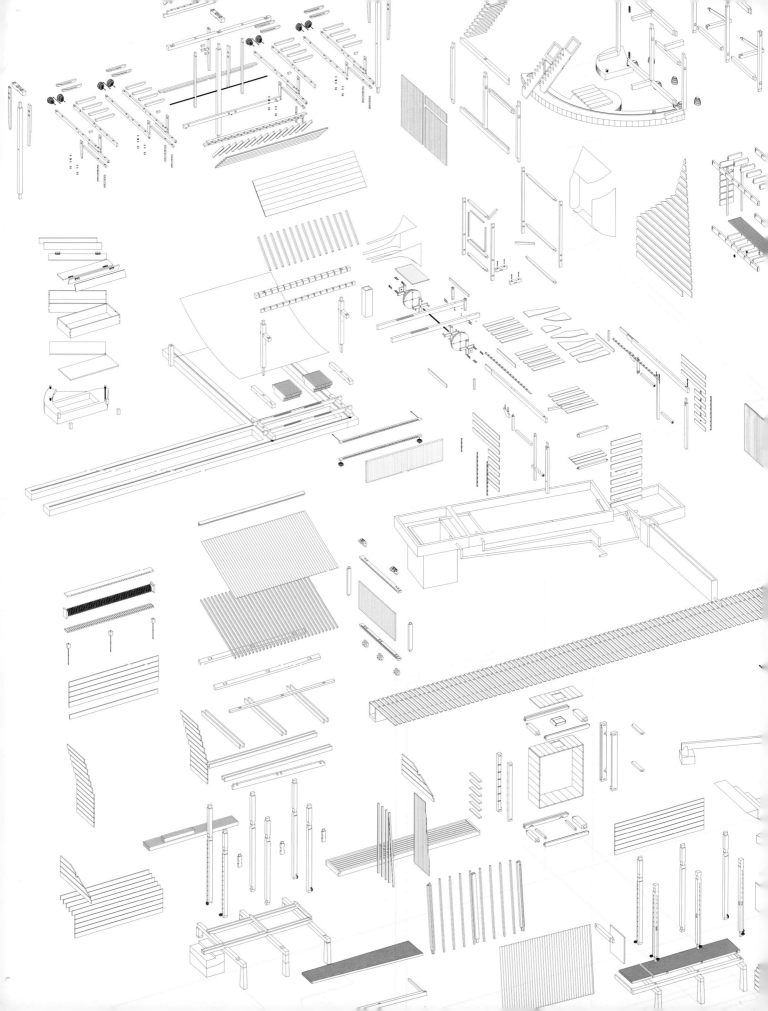

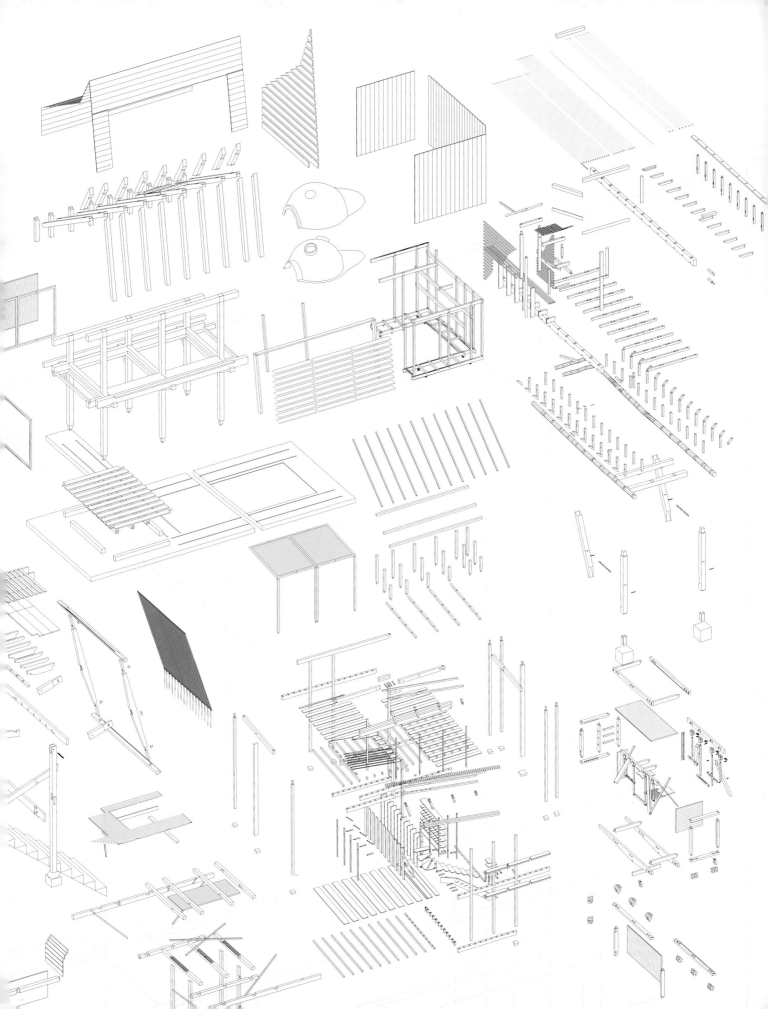

Reading Chairs

Kazuyuki Hanada
Ken Mineta
Ei Onda
Ryu Tsuchiya
Masanori Watanabe

Marco Djermaghian
Annika Grafweg
Takeshi Hayatsu
Satoshi Isono
Taishi Kanemura
Rumi Kubokawa
Yasuyuki Kurosawa
Andreas Lang
Shinji Miyagawa
Yoko Murakami
Harumi Naganuma
Kayoko Nagata
Kenta Nomura
Masato Odakura
Akiko Ohtomo
Keiichi Saito
Tobi Schneidler
Shibboleth Shechter
Miho Suzuki
Asao Tokoro
Masataka Tsuboi
Jan Pietje Witt
Tatsuya Yabusaki
Yuichi Yamanaka

Shin Egashira

Special Guests
Tadahiko Higuchi
Fram Kitagawa
Hitoshi Watanabe

The reality of the landscape is changed by the perceptions of time and memory that lie hidden beneath it. In Koshirakura temporality affects the land in three specific ways: through the slow process of land formation, the steady seasonal cycle of farming and the rapid fluctuation in the price of rice. The topography reveals traces of the repetitive patterns of cultivation, emerging from – and submersed in – the forces of nature and the shifting economy of the region's agriculture.

The workshop began with a reading of the landscape based on its textural details. By extracting geomorphological codes we were able to see the direct link between the forms of the land and the forms of its inhabitation and cultivation – such as *chumon tsukuri* (thatched-roof house), *yokoido* (horizontal well-system) and *mabu* (earth-cutting technique for irrigation).

As an initial experiment we made a series of small models that were intended somehow to fit this landscape into our hands. We wanted to make a souvenir for someone close, like a grandmother living abroad, that would allow them to experience the landscape by touch rather than sight, in combination with narratives in the form of picture-less postcards.

Sequentially these non-scale, or perhaps one-to one, textural models speak about various conditions of the local economy as they are defined by the surface patterns carved out by geology. They reveal the process of negotiation between its sedimentary layers and natural climatic forces, showing how, for instance, the varying proportions of clay and sand give rise to different behaviours, switching from solid to fragile in response to moisture levels, weathering and degree of slope.

Following a similar pattern, each of these small models begins to link to the others to create readings of the land.

In the second project 22 chairs were made for different locations, each chosen for its potential to open our bodies to the experiences offered by the hidden codes of the land. Later these sites were linked by the creation of a new footpath that connected the interior and exterior terrains of the community via segments of old and disused paths. A map was drawn as a guide, allowing one to follow this route and discover the series of hidden chairs for reading the landscape.

Opposite: Chairs for reading the landscape.

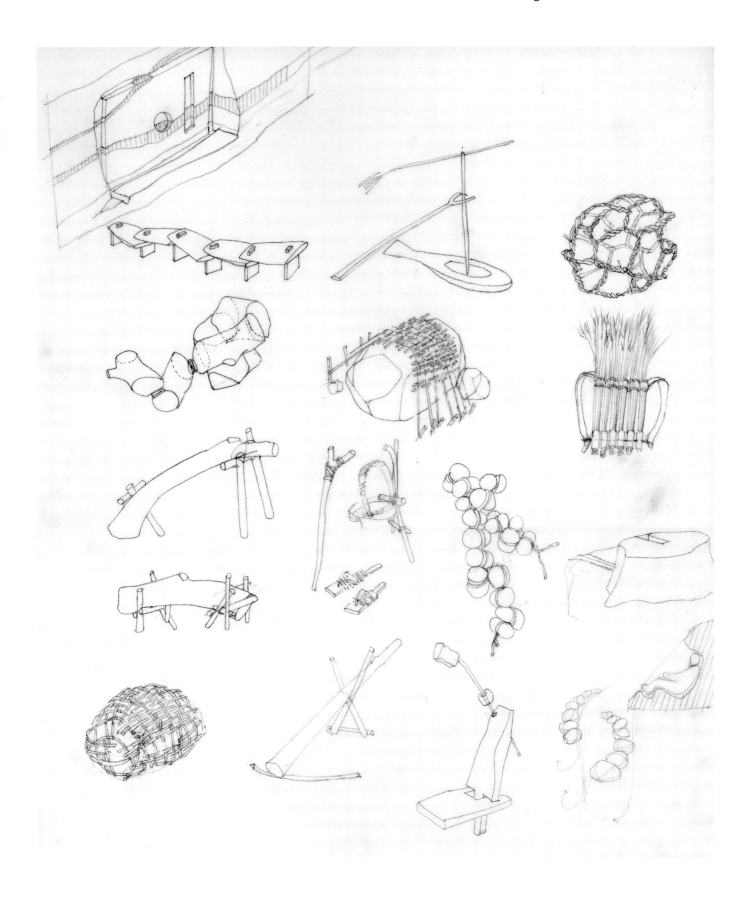

Right:
A series of textural models –
landscape experienced through
our hands. They include a map of
the village woven in straw to show
various textural densities and a
model of a house broken down
into its structural components
of tree, river stone, clay and rice
(straw and paper).

Overleaf:
Textural models, including a
mud-rock water container and
a series of clay blocks as pieces
of land, wrapped, tied, curved,
compressed, hollowed out and
pierced.

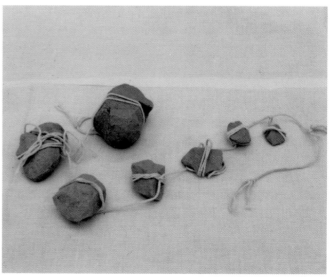

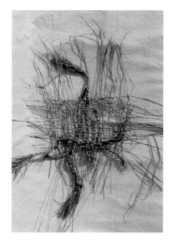

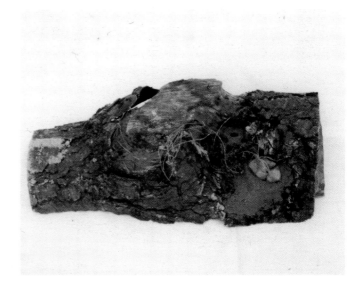

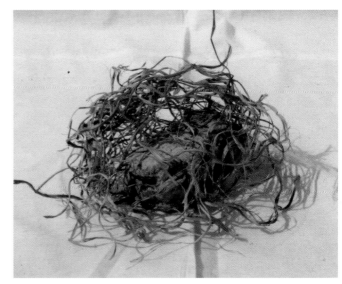

Left: A 'fish' chair that plays on the delicate balance between water, rice field and earth. The piece provides a rare sitting position by the river, where you can rest your feet on stones and feel the flow of the water around them. While sitting, your nose may get tickled by the end of the rice straw. Leaning back, lying down on the stones taken from the riverbed, you can listen to the sounds of the stream and the rice field behind. The fish is floating, responding to the changes of flowing water. (Rumi Kubokawa and Andreas Lang)

Opposite: This work exposes the idea of time that exists within the landscape. A portrait of the land, it invites people to sit between the surface of the ground and the depth of the geological strata. (Masataka Tsuboi)

Centre and bottom left: A family of six benches were made from *nemagari* timber (rejected by the forestry industry). They were placed along the traces of an old path, then existing in fragments, to re-establish a line of visual structure in the scenery of the landscape. (Kenta Nomura)

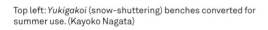

Top left: *Yukigakoi* (snow-shuttering) benches converted for summer use. (Kayoko Nagata)

Bottom left: A mud-rock that had fallen in a landslide was turned into a seat by wrapping it to preserve it against drying and crumbling away. (Tatsuya Yabusaki)

Top right: Drainage was installed at the lower edge of the village to prevent a 200-year-old tree stump from rotting away. A section of the stump was planed so that it revealed 200 growth rings as a surface to sit on and touch. (Harumi Naganuma)

Bottom right: A pumpkin was used as a mould for a seat made out of vines. (Annika Grafweg)

Bottom left: A woven nest for playing inside the bushes rolls along the hidden topography. (Mie Suzuki)

Bottom right: Tree observatory for foresters. (Yasu Kurosawa)

Top left and right: The rucksack is about half the size of a tatami mat and can be used as a rocking tatami as well as a seat/bag for a collector who wishes to explore the landscape around Koshirakura. The materials used were all found in the village – corrugated iron, bicycle tubes, rope and bundles of harvested rice from the field. Their use reflects still-apparent traditional building techniques, as well as the recent influx of mass-produced materials. (Tobi Schneidler)

Climbing, walking, sitting, sliding body gadgets that enable one to complete a 1 km journey through a section of the landscape. (Shinji Miyagawa)

Mud-stone mat: Mud-stones connected by a rice rope create a line, a surface to step on, an object to sit on. (Takeshi Hayatsu and Shibboleth Shechter)

1997 Bus Shelter

Yasuyuki Kurosawa
Ruth Lonsdale
Ken Mineta
Ei Onda
Asao Tokoro
Ryu Tsuchiya
Masanori Watanabe

Takako Hasegawa
Kristina Hertel
Nimit Kamder
Freven Lim
Emu Masuyama
Hiroko Ogura
Sanjeev Sharma
Tmoko Sugimoto
Tatsuo Takayama
John Tyrrell
Haruna Yamada

Toshiaki Higuchi
Yasuhiro Hoshina

Shin Egashira

How big is the village? Where does it begin and end? The size of the village on the official map must be very different from the size of the landscape created in people's minds. These landscapes cannot be measured in two dimensions; they occupy the space- and time-scales of the collective memory of the village.

We asked the villagers to identify the points at which the village begins. Some responses were based on childhood memories of the limits beyond which their parents had told them not to stray, whilst others clearly pointed out the mountain ridge from which the entire village can be overlooked. We tried to collect these individual recognitions and memories, and to sort them according to topography and time. The result was a series of maps: a map of lost paths; a map of sounds, a map of the shifting colours of the landscape, a map of childhood memories associated with cherry trees, and many more. These maps were then overlaid upon a map made the previous year.

This year, a local bus route started to serve the village twice a day. When we discussed the construction of a new local artefact, it seemed obvious that there should be a Bus Shelter where both children and grandparents could be protected from heavy snow and wind on winter mornings. Referring to the map made previously, several locations were identified as possible sites. This project presented an opportunity not only to mark the terminus of the bus route but also to create a new entrance to the village.

The structure is a collage of detailed representations of the landscape. The various ground textures were imprinted on clay tablets. The *yukigakoi* (snow-scattering timber planks), which provide protection during the winter, can be taken down and moved to a site across the road, where they form an open bench from spring to autumn. Another large structure is also detached from the shelter during this time and presents the views and colours of each season as if pictures in a frame. In its spring position, it frames the colour of the earth as it first emerges from beneath the melting snow. In summer it frames the high point of the spring water. In the winter, contained within the wall of the *yukigakoi*, it becomes a platform onto which children can climb, allowing them to see the entire village covered in snow.

The angles of the Bus Shelter roof were determined by the angle at which the snow settles. Its transparency allows sunlight into the sheltered space even when it is covered by snow (often to a depth of two to four metres). Each facade is aligned with the autumn sunset, when the sun is at its most intense shade of orange. Sandstone collected from the Shinano river was used for the floor and *yukigakoi* details.

Through a combination of openness and the intimacy of its interior, the Bus Shelter registers seasonal changes. It reveals the process of its formation, as well as aspects of the landscape. Some details were left to be articulated later; others were intentionally fragile. In both instances the point was to keep the community involved with the space by making it one that requires maintenance.

Opposite: Bus Shelter in closed and open positions.

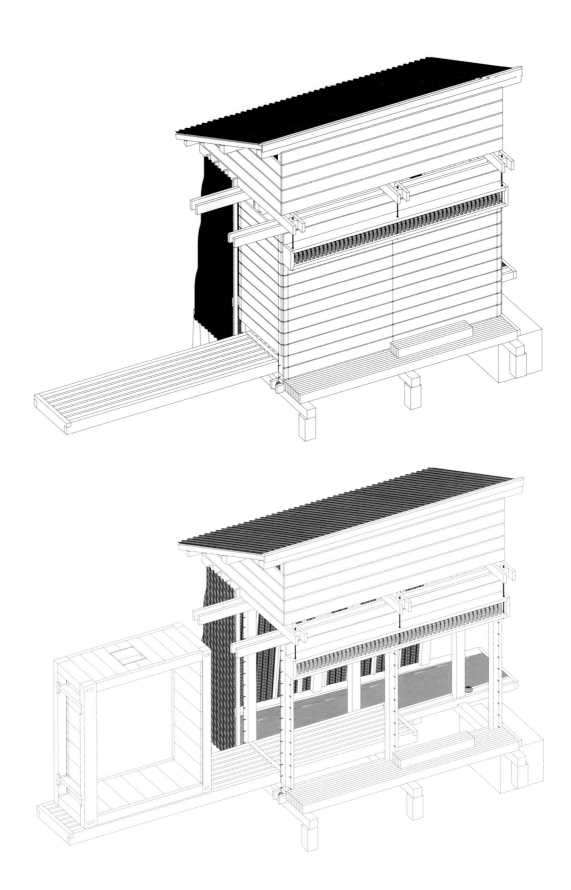

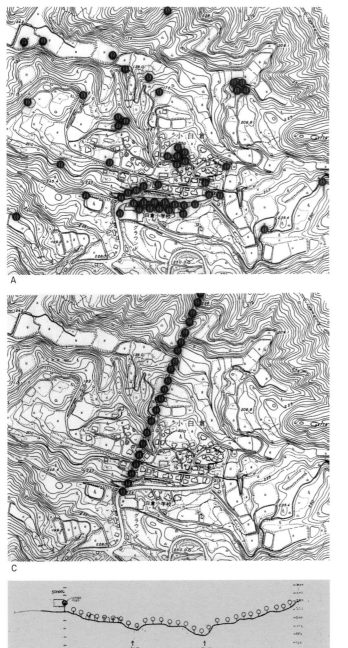

A

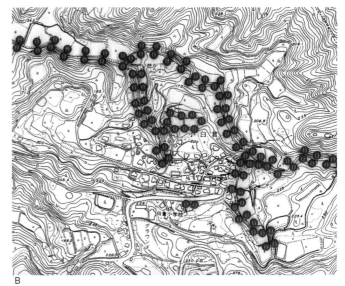

B

C

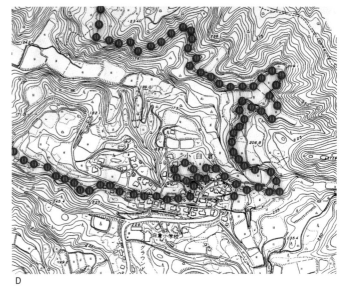

D

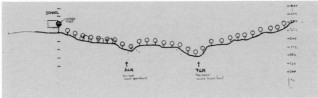

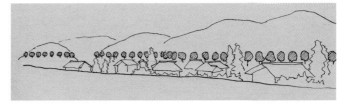

Above and opposite top: Proposals for planting 300 cherry trees.

A   Follow a contour-line at the same height as the rooftops of the village. In springtime the edge of the village is articulated as a pink blossom line for a period of one week.
B   Follow streams of water irrigation.
C   Follow the section-line where the level changes are the most significant, so the cherry trees will start blossoming at the lower levels and gradually rise up the hill, creating a seasonal clock that indicates time by the length of the glowing colour.

D   Use each tree as a marker for the memory spots of villagers.
E   Overlay new trees on top of the existing alignment of old cherry trees planted 300 years ago along the then main path through the village.

Opposite below: Map to indicate the various sounds of hidden streams running along the side of the road.

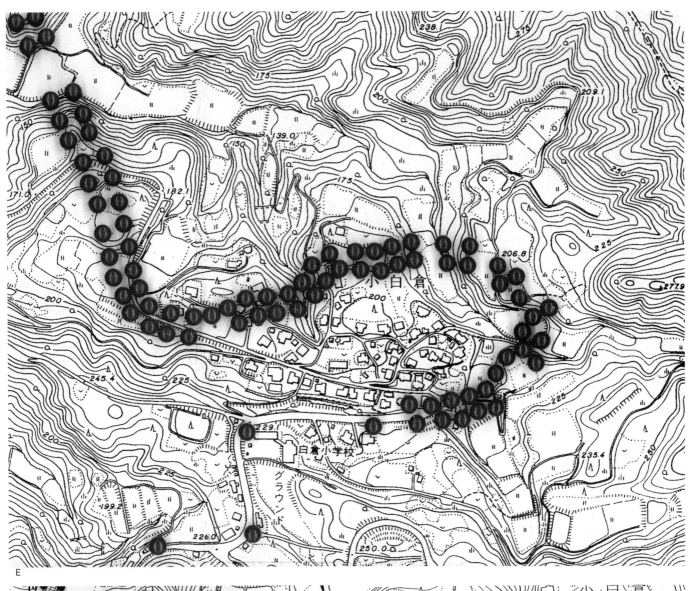

E

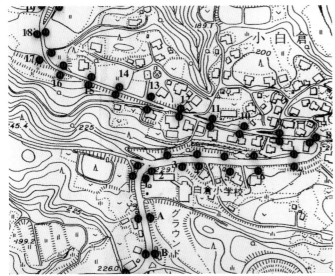

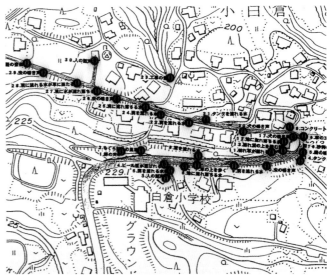

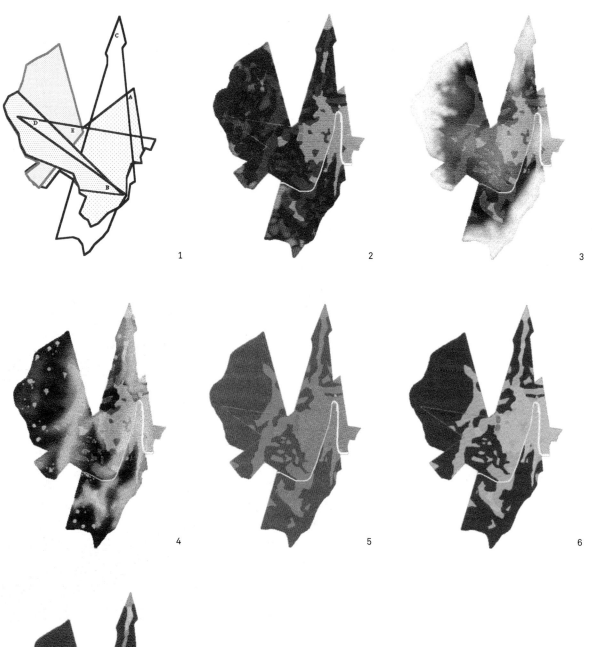

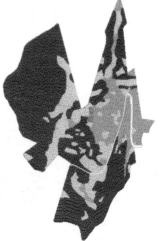

1 Overlaid plans of vistas that define the edge of the village
as it exists in the individual memory of villagers. A new map
of Koshirakura indicates how big the village is.

2-7 Maps that indicate seasonal changes in patterns of
colours, based upon existing habitats for trees and
vegetation. 2 Early autumn. 3 Early winter. (The all-white
mid-winter map is not shown.) 4 Early spring. 5 Late spring.
6 Early summer. 7 Late summer.

Winter   When December comes, Koshirakura is submerged under snow. The Bus Shelter is wrapped with snow-shuttering for the long winter season and can be entered only from the east side. People waiting inside can recognise the approach of the bus by changes in the sounds and light coming through the clay-tile clerestory.

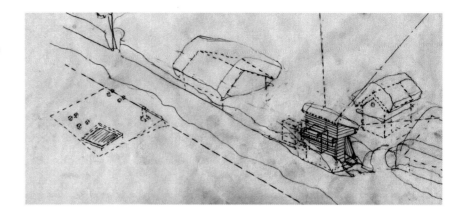

Spring   As winter gradually gives way to spring, the first patch of earth appears under the melting snow. This indicates the time is ready for the snow-shuttering bench to be carried out to its summer site. Water replaces snow as the most significant feature of the view: sitting on the bench, people can savour the thawing of the earth as well as the musical sound of running water.

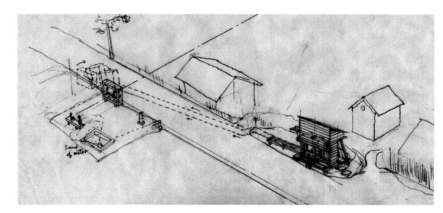

Summer   As the cherry trees blossom, the frame which has been enclosed within the Bus Shelter is carried out and set in its summer position. From either side, the structure frames the view as if it were a picture. The flowing water and the fish in the pond assuage the discomfort of waiting for a bus in the heat of summer.

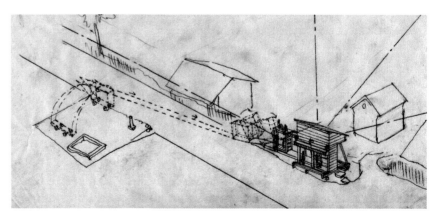

Autumn   After the Maple Tree Festival the frame and bench are carried back into the winter structure. The frame can be pulled outside on warmer days, providing a place for locals to chat as well as an open-air stall for selling vegetables.

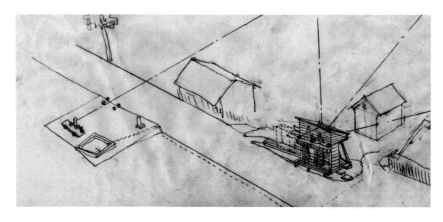

Top: Textures were borrowed from either side of the main road and transferred to a series of clay tablets. These were later fired and made into an archive/window through which light penetrates to emphasise each texture that can be seen and touched from inside the bus stop during the winter period when the snow-shuttering is up.

Right: River-worn stones were gathered from the Shinano and used as interior flooring and as weights for a series of wires fastening the snow-shuttering against the columns.

Far right and below: As the bench slides into the shelter where it is stored during winter, it creates a small attic space below the light roof. A little opening enables a child to climb up and view the village across the deep snow.

Right: Erection of main frame on site.

Far right and below: Sliding bench details.

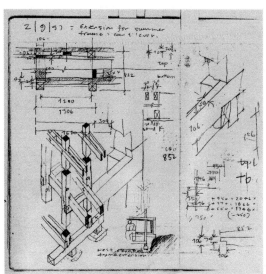

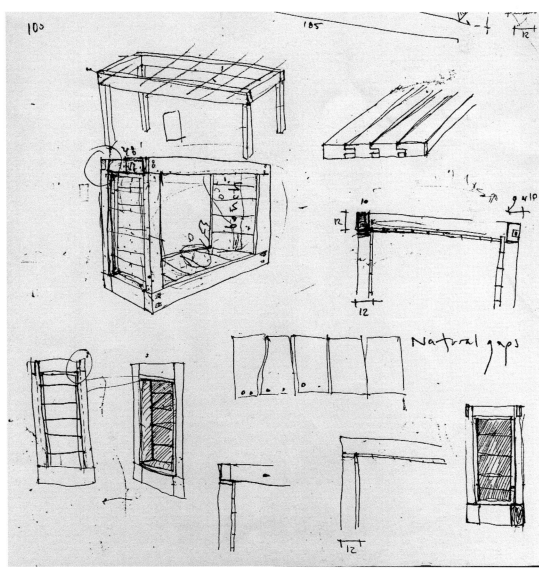

Top left: Sliding bench in the summer position. From behind it works as a picture frame for viewing the first snow-melting spot in the village.

Centre left: From the front one can see a second seating place behind, where cold water from the horizontal well comes to the surface.

Bottom left: Sliding bench in autumn.

Below: There is a small window in the side of the bench through which the bus stop can be seen. As the bench flips 90 degrees to come inside the Bus Shelter, this opening becomes an access hatch to the attic space.

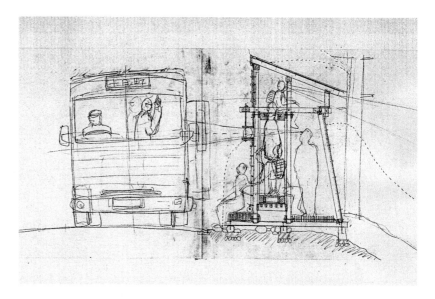

Top: Sketch section examining the relationships between the structure and different eye-levels.

Centre and bottom: A bus arriving and leaving for the first time in the history of Koshirakura.

Bus Shelter in winter and summer.

Ruth Lonsdale
Ken Mineta
Masanori Watanabe

Yanko Apostolov
Tania Bahtia
Samina Choudhry
Marco Djermaghian
Emilio Garcia
Takako Hasegawa
Yasuhiro Hayashi
Koichiro Ioka
Satoshi Isono
Zahra Kalantarian
Clara Kraft
Kwan Guan Lee
Stephan Loeffler
Emu Masuyama
Shinji Miyagawa
Yoko Murakami
Cezar L Negrete
Wan Shophopanich
Junichi Tamura
Wei Tseng
Kazuya Yamazaki
Kai Ping Yang

Hiroyasu Kurono
Yutaka Yokoyama

Shin Egashira

The theme for 1998 was 'the body in play with the environment'. The prefectural government of Niigata had initiated a plan for regenerating the grounds of the abandoned school by turning them into a communal park. The Kawanishi administration wished to revise the initial plan by devising a process that would allow local identity and local needs to be reflected in its design. In doing so they hoped to capture the interest and attention of the villagers. The message was: 'This is a park which need not be sophisticated, but could only be possible in Koshirakura'.

This year we decided to work directly, using the school grounds as our drawing board, our shovels, pickaxes and spades as our pens and pencils, and our buckets and wheelbarrows as our erasers and scalpels. The school grounds are the largest area of flat land in the locality. Hidden by a hill, they appeared to have been forgotten since the school closed. We inscribed relationships between the body and the landscape. We mapped ground conditions according to the softness and wetness of the land: the north is an exposed hard clay surface, the south a compound ground that is soft and soggy. At the edges, along the hillside, the land had become a shallow swamp of stagnant water that smelled of rotting plants.

The mappings of previous years allowed us to rethink the location of the grounds. Lines were cut into the ground to mark the way towards key locations: two viewpoints from which the whole village can be overlooked, a 300-year-old cherry tree that features strongly in the awareness of the villagers, and the point at which the sun sets on 15 September (when it is supposed to be most vivid). These lines had to be distinct enough to be identified from the points to which they refer. Readings of the saturation of the soil and the direction of the slope also influenced the articulation of the cuts. Functioning as a small irrigation system, these incisions drain off water so that textural differences can be established (this is analogous to the cultivation of the terraced rice field using the *mabu* earth-cutting technique).

Children develop their relationships to the outside world through encounters with objects – 'toys' (for them any object can serve as a toy). By playing with toys they shift from the imaginary to an idea of reality. Having borrowed this idea of the transitional object from psychology, we considered how we might apply it to the relationship between the transitional body of the land and the stages at which objects emerge as agents enabling us to transform our idea of place. Was a reversal of this transition possible? How might the real ground be transformed through the imagination (or lack of memory) in a child's mind?

We began by making 'fictional' toys, borrowing ideas from traditional agricultural tools or domestic appliances. We played a game, taking the series of toys made during the first week of the workshop and improvising a logic to link and position them. We arranged ourselves into six teams, to develop and construct full-scale models of the 'body in play with the land'. The names of the structures (which also became the names of the teams) were invented through games: Slow Window, Harmonious Local Materials, Quiet Stone, Weather Accommodation Deck, Wet Projection, Clear Viewing Structure.

Four lines, six structures of behaviour and maps from previous years became objects to be drawn, inscribed and constructed on the face of the school grounds. It became a playground where, under the summer rain, we played hard in the mud. Some structures were completed then and others were prepared for future evolution.

Opposite: Slow Window in its various configurations.

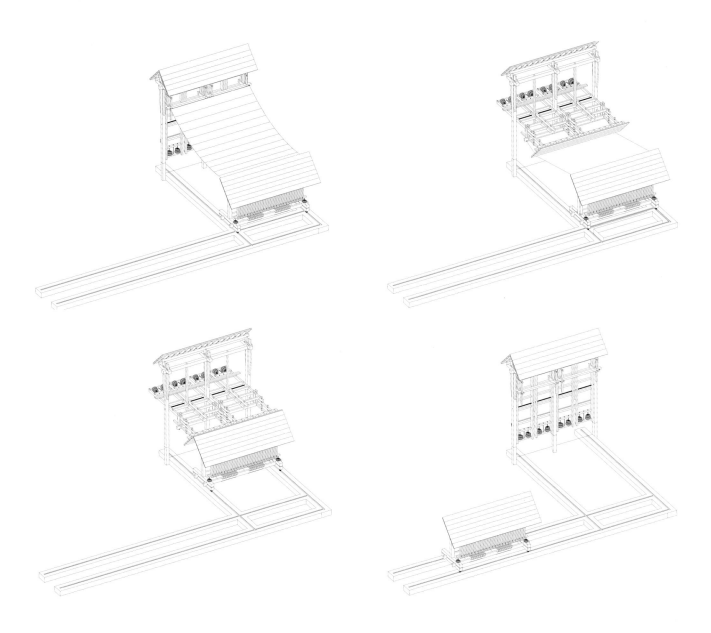

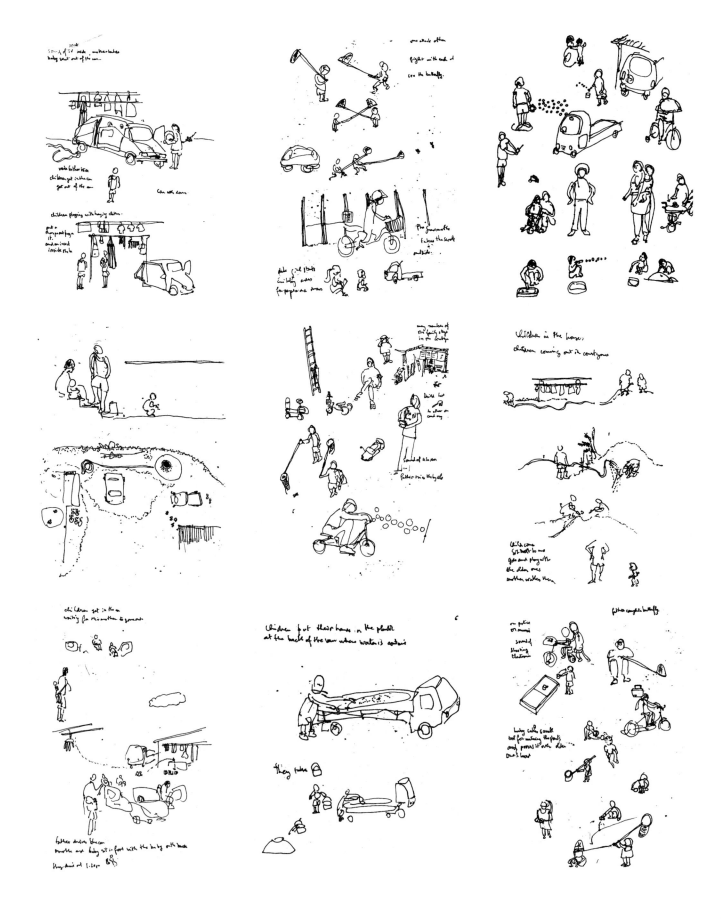

Opposite: Pictograms showing existing local tools, activities and locations.

Toys, from top to bottom, left to right: Wind-powered drawing machine; series of micro-windmills; how to wear a Quiet Stone; plough for listening to the sound of the soil; musical rice-separator; pebble-sorter; musical instrument.

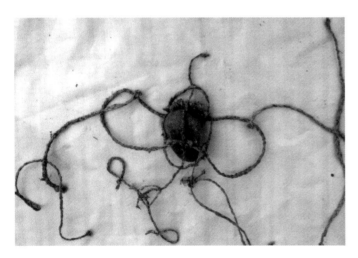

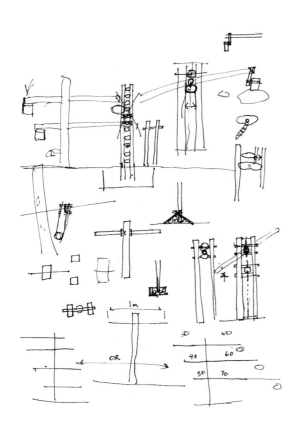

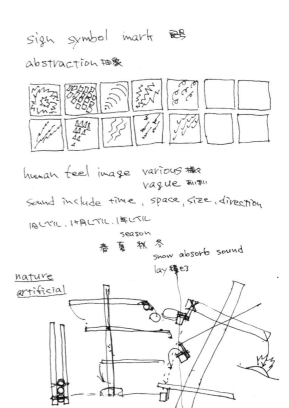

sign symbol mark 記号

abstraction 抽象

human feel image various 様々

vague あいまい

sound include time, space, size, direction

旧しくて、現代しくて、新しくて

season

春夏秋冬

snow absorb sound

lay 積もる

nature

artificial

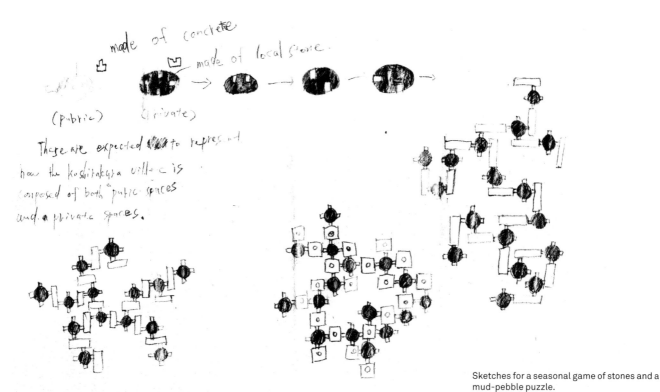

↳ made of concrete

↳ made of local stone.

(public)   (private)

These are expected to represent how the Kushitakura village is composed of both public spaces and a private spaces.

Sketches for a seasonal game of stones and a mud-pebble puzzle.

Top: Initial plan of the site, indicating zones with higher degrees of softness/wetness or stagnant/ overgrown areas caused by the lack of surface drainage. Lines of coordinates were taken from the new map of the village from 1997 and used as visual axes to link the site with various viewpoints at the edge of the village, Later on those axes became actual cuts in the ground, serving as water channels.

Bottom: A site model was initially made in the form of a game board at the centre of the site, using actual materials condensed from the surroundings.

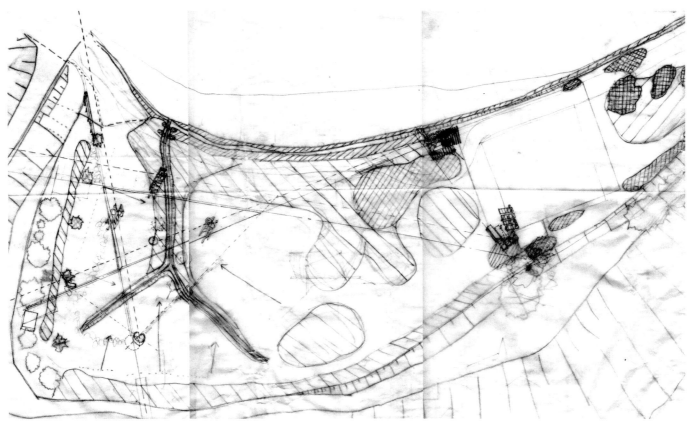

Opposite, clockwise
from top left:
Clear Viewing Structure
along one of the cuts;
first, second and third
cuts; foundation works
In progress.

Right, from top:
Earthworks in progress
(for the Harmonious
Local Materials Bench
and Slow Window);
marking the position
of the Weather Accom-
modation Platform.

Left: Slow Window under construction.

Below left: Weather Accommodation Platform. A rammed earth wall built upon concrete and stone foundations insulates a room so it can be used as a cold store. It follows the same principles as the *yukimuro* (snow room), a traditional way of storing food and sake that insulates snow to preserve it over the summer. The locals hoped to chill bottles of sake and beer for drinking after croquet practice.

Opposite: Preparing the foundations for the Weather Accommodation Platform's mud wall.

Left, from top: Harmonious Local Materials Bench in half-open and closed positions; Harmonious Local Materials sample box.

Opposite: Harmonious Local Materials Bench in open and closed positions.

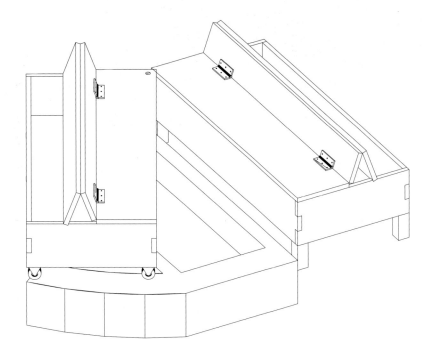

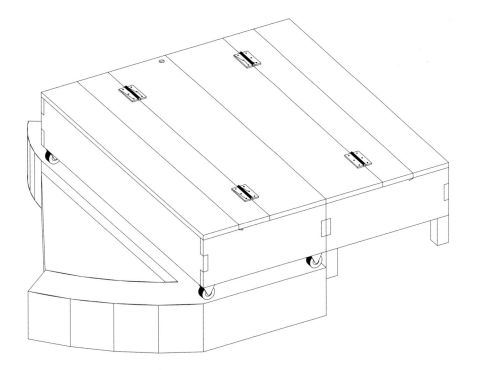

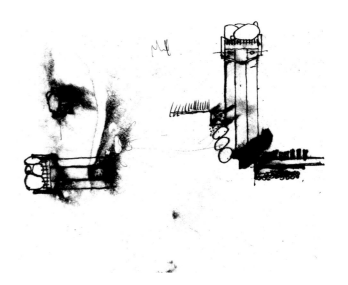

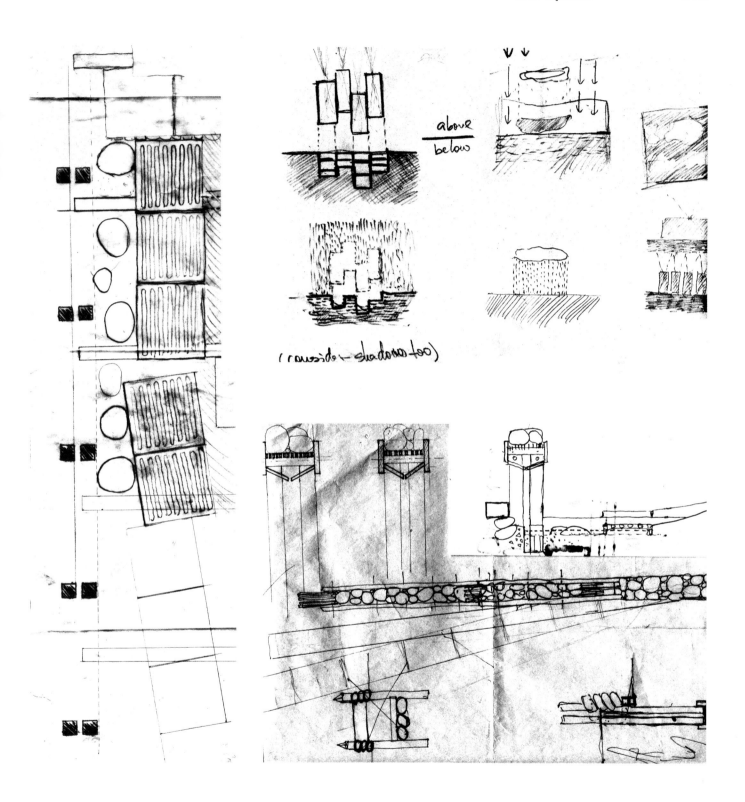

Opposite: Drainage system under construction. The precast concrete paving slabs were rejects donated by Nagata Concrete Manufacturing Co. Ltd., and the river-worn stones were hand-picked from the Shinano – a local stonemason sliced some of them.

Above: Drawings and sketches of the Wet Projection.

Top: Body imprint sequence (Quiet Stone).

Bottom: Body/earth-casting process.

 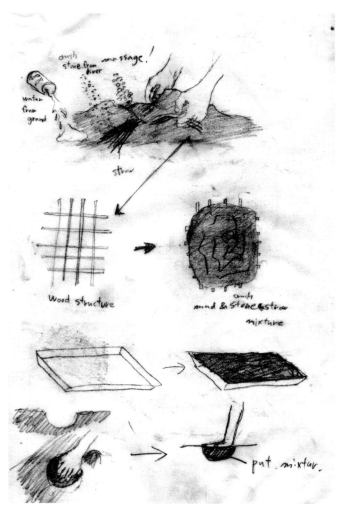

Top: Body/earth-casting process.

Bottom: How to mix mud, straw, soba and water to make a mould (Quiet Stone).
See the diary entries for 1998 for more on soba.

Overview of groundworks, phase one.

One of three Quiet Stones positioned along the park axis.

1999　Azumaya

Hitoshi Ihara
Ruth Lonsdale
Masanori Watanabe

Ludwig Abache
Yanko Apostolov
Phoebe Dakin
Marco Djermaghian
Hideaki Fujita
Marta Belem Gomez
Carolin Hinne
With assistance from
the Igawa Corporation
Koichiro Ioka
Stella Kamba
Martand Kosula
Aoi Kume
Kazuomi Kurashina
Patric Lam
Sam Liu
Shuji Mizukami
Wan Sophopanich
Yasushi Takahashi
With the expertise
of the Takahashi
Construction Company
and Chief Carpenter
Kamimura
Razvan Mosnag Teifil
Naomi Yamada
Kazuya Yamazaki
Kai Ping Yang
Bibiana Zapf

Shin Egashira

The Azumaya (summer pavilion, arbour) is the archetype of the traditional garden hut – a refuge from the sun and the rain, a covered space rather than an enclosed interior. Traditional rules govern these small buildings. They should have no walls (to ensure a free flow of air, water and energy); their form should be asymmetrical (since the space under a symmetrical roof is traditionally reserved for the upper classes); and they should not rest on four columns (to avoid any parallel with the space under a four-legged animal).

Following last year's workshop, the local administration asked for a specific design for a new Azumaya so they could apply to the prefectural government for funds that are allocated for individual regeneration projects in local towns. The basic design of the Azumaya was made during the winter of 1998/99 based on the gathering of ideas and details from previous years. A set of drawings was produced in order to secure planning permission. Extra materials were allocated for the ground works, such as sandstone, cherry trees, turf, sand, cement and aggregate. Machines and tools for basic landscaping and construction were provided. The project went out to tender. By its nature, it required the transgression of several conventions: the construction process was to involve a collaboration between the workshop and the contractor; apart from the basic structure, several design details would be left 'open' to allow for adjustment during the workshop, and students were to have the opportunity to learn the techniques of joinery from the chief carpenter during the timber assembly. The contractor would have to agree not only to work within the timescale of the workshop (in order to allow the collaboration) but also to be legally responsible for its timely completion. Only one contractor tendered for so demanding, yet so very small, a construction.

In the first week, we documented the interior and exterior landscape of the village with pinhole cameras (made by hand from cardboard boxes). This allowed us to re-see the space as volumes of light and shadow. Any clear distinction between the figure and the ground was erased. The images were developed in a temporary darkroom created in the bathroom of the school building. The theme was 'the figure and the ground' – the face of the land and the landscape reflected upon the faces of people. Following this first week of documentation, four teams were formed, each with its own programme.

Team 1: Collaborate with the contractor on the construction of the Azumaya. Learn how to construct traditional timber joints from the chief carpenter (the two sliding benches could then be assembled by the team without the use of nails or metal fixings).

Team 2: Begin the landscaping by shifting surplus earth from the excavation of the foundations. Set out new textural plans over the preliminary layer and positions inscribed during the previous year. The materials provided were five cubic metres of sandstone, 300 square metres of turf, 12 cherry trees and the leftover earth from the foundation works, as well as the discarded playground structures. Tools included a small power-shovel digger, two wheelbarrows, some gardening hand tools and two mini-trucks.

Team 3: Rethink and develop the idea of the Slow Window (inherited from last year's work). Build over the structure made last year to create a rest area for the adjacent croquet court that the elderly use for team practice in the summer.

Team 4: Complete the Wet Projection begun last summer. (This team was made up of students who had started the project the previous year.)

Opposite: The Azumaya can be both an open and an enclosed space.

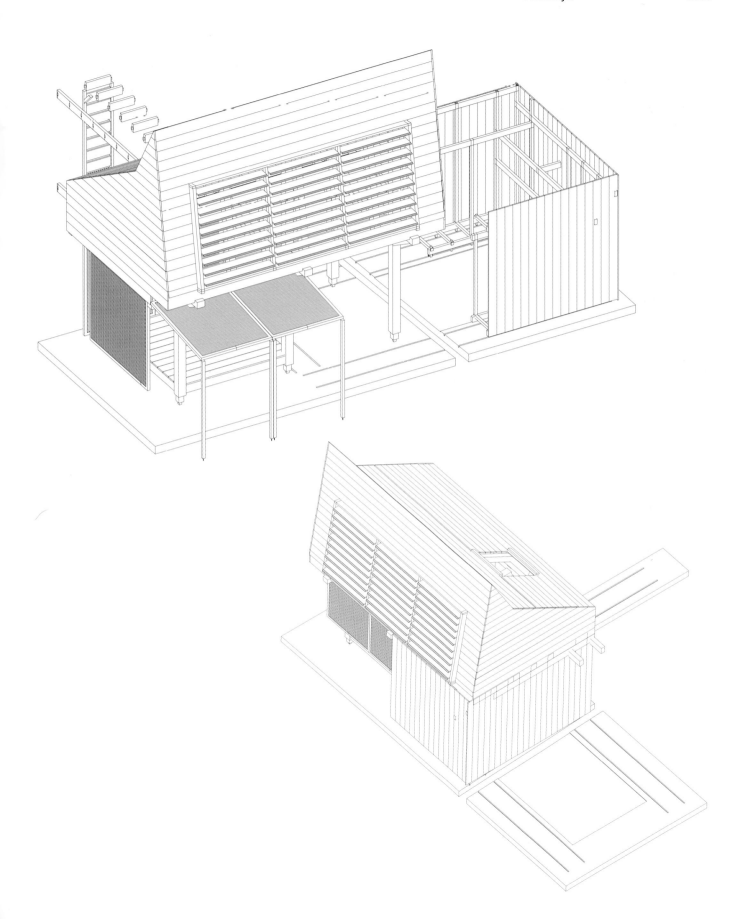

Opposite and above: A series of cardboard pinhole cameras.

Documenting the interior and exterior landscape of the village.

Above: Haruo and Noriko Eguchi's living room, 21 August.
Below: Kitabori residence, 17 August.

Opposite top: School entrance, 16 August. Opposite below: Akiko Tanaka and her mother in their vegetable garden, 17 August.

The participants in the workshop included 16 students from the AA and four students of architecture and fine art from Japanese universities (none of whom had any technical skills in the making of timber joints, ferrocement construction, laying a lawn, foundation works or roofing). They were joined by some skilled local people who worked alongside them for two weeks until the morning of the Maple Tree Festival (which coincided with the completion of the first phase of the park).

The spatial characteristics of the Azumaya were composed of language, details and textures extracted from previous years' structures. Although the formulae of the roof angles and other attendant details were learned from vernacular traditions for dealing with snow, such features achieve their unique spatial significance from spring to autumn, when the absence of snow generates excess volumes of space.

Above the structure of the Azumaya is a roof space that can be used by children for sleepovers during the summer. In winter the depth of this dark enclosed volume registers the accumulation of snow – the layers of snow are represented by slits of reflected light. The colours of each season permeate the light entering through the north-facing *akaritori* (clerestory) louvres: the green of summer, the red leaves of autumn, the white of winter snow and, in spring, the pink of the blossoms on the cherry tree directly in line with the louvres. The apertures can be adjusted; so too can a sliding bench, a second frame-like structure and a screen. Relationships between the benches and the main structure can be reconfigured to allow for activities such as karaoke parties, koto concerts and tea ceremonies. When the benches are drawn in to enclose the structure, the space is smaller and more intimate – suitable for private meetings. The space communicates both enclosure and openness.

Slow Window demonstrates a simple transition of space (also deployed in the Azumaya) by turning the emphasis of the structure from horizontal to vertical. In winter it closes into an almost vertical plane buried under the snow. As the snow melts in spring it slides before turning and unfolding into the enlarged space.

Moon Hill used a structure left over from the site's days as a playground as a framework for the ferrocement construction of a grotto-like space, which was then buried under a mound of earth. The topography of this hill was tailored by different positions of bodies – sitting, lying down, stargazing, anticipating the full moon of September or the sunset. Small openings allow various elements of the land to be glimpsed from inside the hill, which becomes an enclosed 'fort' where children play.

Two bridges, Overpass and Platform, appear detached from the Azumaya and the Slow Window. Yet they are connected at a distance – marking points of entrance and the intersection of visual axes. As you approach, sequences of views reveal themselves through angles, level changes and intervals of details.

Wet Projection is a small elongated waterway that provides drainage. It collects water from the roof of the Azumaya and from the four axes that were cut during the previous year. The channel allows a strip of sky to be reflected onto the ground, and the sound of running water can be heard at the main entrance to the area.

A section through the Azumaya and a cherry tree. The movement of leaves will be registered as flickering reflected light inside, penetrating through the north-facing shuttering – green in the summer, pink in the spring.

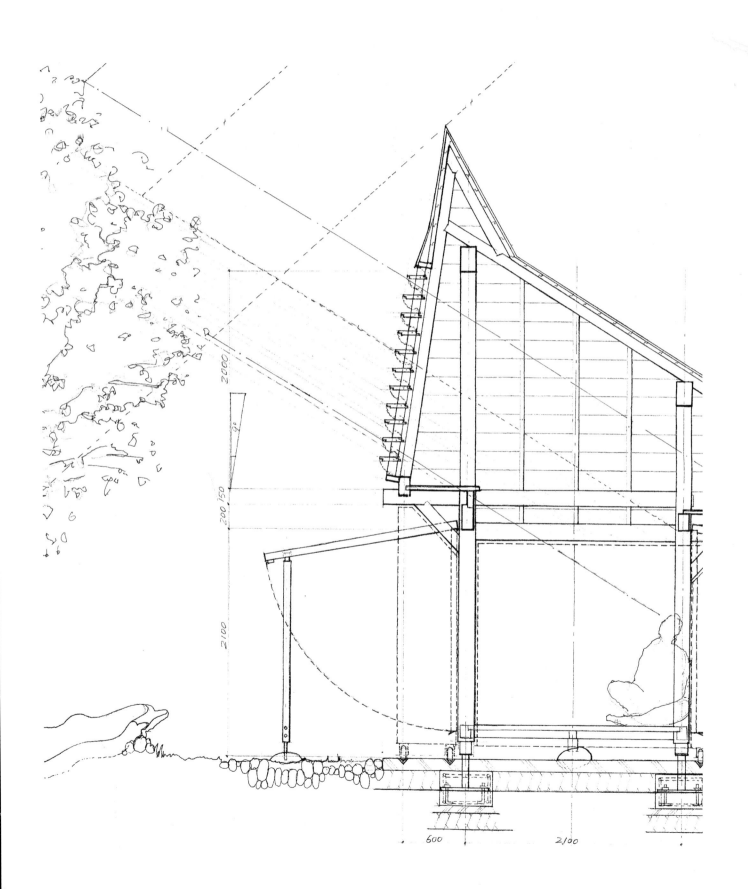

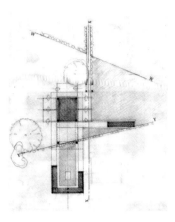

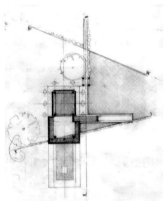

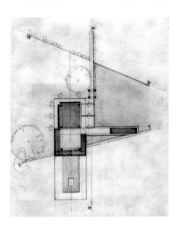

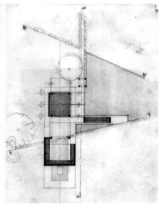

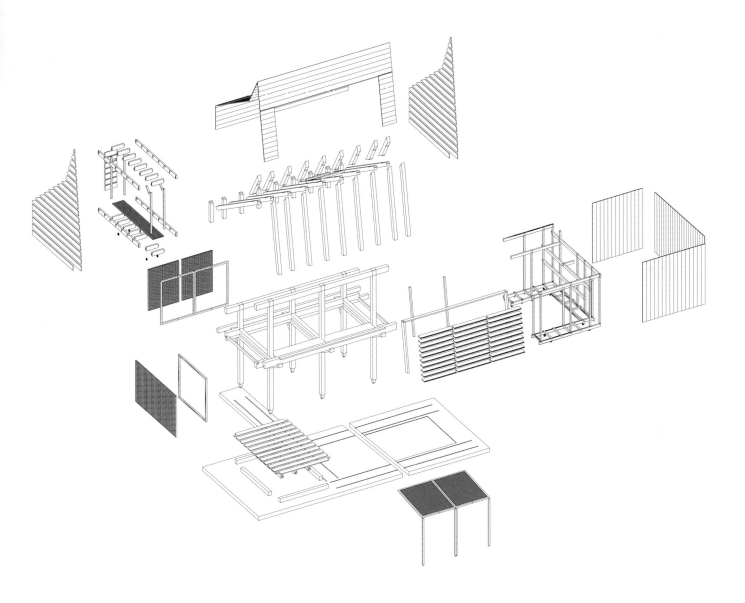

Opposite: The enclosed space of the Azumaya unfolds and transforms into a series of
spatial components. The plan sequence shows the transformation, from top to bottom:
into BBQ setting, intimate meetings, tearoom and karaoke stage.

Above: Exploded axonometric of the Azumaya

Views through, from and within the Azumaya, with construction process shown below.

In spring, when the snow begins to melt, the Azumaya re-emerges.

Sketch plans and details of
groundworks and Overpass
bridge/seat.

Opposite: Groundworks, phase 2
in progress. Includes
embankment complete with
planting of 20 cherry trees,
Overpass and Platform bridges,
Slow Window, Moon Hill and
Wet Projection.

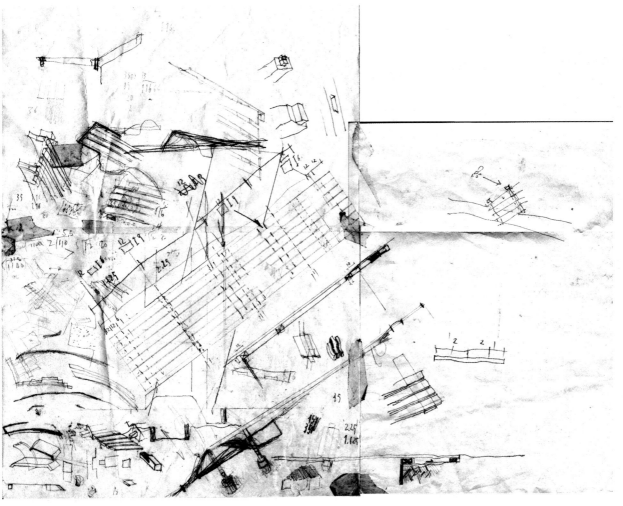

Slow Window roofing works and structure half-open for picnics and gatherings.

Opposite: Slow Window fully closed for winter, and about to be fully open for a croquet match.

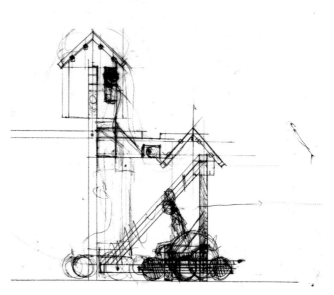

Above: The Slow Window provides a shady place to rest.

Opposite: The Azumaya unfolded.

Erik Alto
Ema Bonafacic
Reem Charif
Maria Cheung
Samina Choudhry
Phoebe Dakin
Koichiro Ioka
Mokoto Kishino
Marie Langen
Julia Mauser
Inigo Minns
Shuji Mizukami
Hoi Chi Ng
Beng-Kiat Phua
Tania Rodriguez
Demosthenis Simatos
Andreas Stehre
Yasushi Takahashi
Kazunori Takeishi

Shin Egashira

In Koshirakura there appears to be no clear line that divides communal and private places, no material borders that define and organise the community as a whole. When paying a visit to the villagers, it is common to walk straight into their house without any warning or calling out of names. You just enter through the sliding doors, take off your shoes and go into the living room and kitchen. If no one is there, you continue upstairs to see if they are taking a nap. Bewildered by this absence of borders, we set out to learn more about how this community is nonetheless so well ordered.

Embedded within Koshirakura we found a few clear organising structures that subdivide the inhabitants into groups. The most important of these is the family group, but the locals also identify each other by *yogou* – the house name rather than the family name. Moreover, the sharing of communal responsibilities and coordination of seasonal activities is organised according to age groups. For example, the elderly group (over 65) is responsible for grass-cutting twice a year, for rope-making during the winter and for the croquet team that represents the village. The senior group (over 40) undertakes snow removal and maintenance works, organises the festival and other events, and handles public affairs outside the community. The position of chief rotates on a yearly basis.

And then there are the various committees: the Fire Security Committee, Rice Harvesting and Planting Committee, Festival Organisation Committee, Biggest Pumpkin Competition Committee, Grass-Cutting Committee, Maple Tree Selection Committee, and so on. These informal groups are very effective at addressing essential issues. A by-product of these collective activities is a series of migratory spaces based on activities rather than permanent divisions marking property boundaries.

We investigated further by looking at the organisation of chores and responsibilities within several families. Every household has an intricate allocation of time for particular tasks, often cyclical in nature, some weekly or daily, others spread over a year. While undertaking several communal jobs, each household continues to grow rice and vegetables. The use of domestic objects, tools and equipment rotates seasonally according to the cycle of rice production, rope-making and other local micro-industries.

To better define these interwoven activities of a domestic and a communal nature, we identified various forms of gathering within the community in terms of their timing and location. The procedures for removing snow, the water networks connecting horizontal wells to each house, pond and rice field and the shared routine maintenance works were all carefully studied. We tried to identify shifting patterns in the way territories of activities are formed along the shared facilities as a network of relations between families, landscape and production. We made maps that indicate changing patterns of locations where people gather informally. For instance, every third Sunday in August since 1997 the elderly group has organised a party with us at the end of the grass-cutting day. This particular event takes place beside the cherry tree at the school entrance defined by a rectangular space made of eight blue tarpaulins. Following the initial research, our main projects attempted to provide new places for social gathering by extending existing shared facilities and communal duties in the village.

Opposite: Exploded axonometric of Watermelon Place showing new plumbing installations.

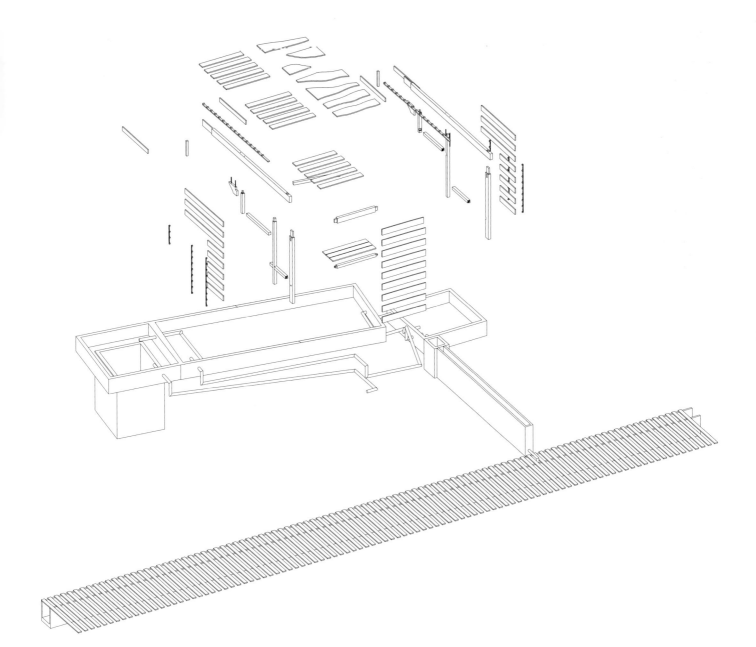

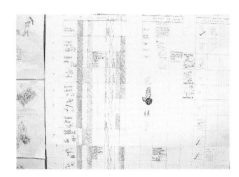
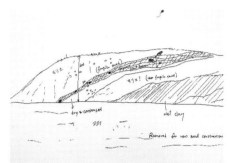
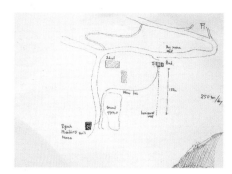

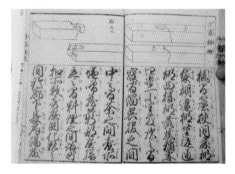
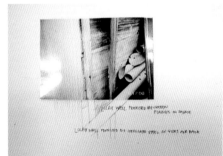
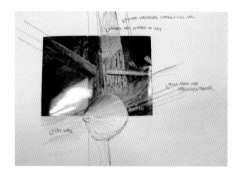

Above from top to bottom, left to right: Seasonal timetable for communal activities; plans and axo of water networks indicated by *yokoido* (horizontal wells), *tateido* (shared reservoirs), carp ponds, snow-melting ponds and paddy-fields; geological samples; handwritten joinery catalogue found in one of the attics; small-scale slack spaces.

Opposite: Study of contents of the villagers' storehouses – a straw-woven traditional raincoat was among the objects found; family-run micro-industry inside a farmhouse (centre right).

Three small objects were made using earth-casting techniques:
Topographical model of the Koshirakura landscape; red bird watching
the village from a tree; water containers.

Preparation and construction of mud wall and *dogama* seat.

Bus Shelter Extension

A regular bus visits the village twice a day and a school bus picks up four children early in the morning and returns them in the afternoon. When the school bus is delayed by snow, the children and their grandparents are often forced to wait for a while inside the Bus Shelter. As the children grew older, however, the room inside became too small.

The team decided to make an extension, complete with a small oven that would provide a heated seat during the winter. The technical inspiration came from the *dogama*, a traditional kitchen oven made with rammed earth. These days *dogamas* are rare. It seemed only Mr Katagiri knew how to build one; even then, he had to ask his father about the ingredients for the mud mixture and the best places to gather the materials.

The recipe for the mud blocks is as follows: sandy clay, chopped rice straw, *shodo* (burnt earth) and bamboo reinforcements. Just as in wine-making, the ingredients are trampled with bare feet in a pool lined with blue tarpaulin sheets. Mud cakes were made in various combinations to test their strength. A big pile of

mud was shaped into a series of little volcano-shaped mounds, topped up with water and left to rest for a few days until the rice straw began to ferment (it was supposed to be checked by tasting).

The ventilation system for the shelter was integrated with the timber structures that replaced three old diagonal columns.

The heated *dogama* seat inside the Bus Shelter.

Watermelon Place in early spring.

Watermelon Place

As a complement to the Bus Shelter extension, which is a winter facility, the team decided to build a cooling place for the summer season. Diagonally across the street from the Bus Shelter is an unused pond for spring water. It is the only remaining feature of Michi's house, which was relocated for road-widening. Our objective was to reopen this forgotten reservoir for public use, as a site for the picture-frame bench, and to reestablish links with the other ponds.

There is a small corner in the village where the main road forks into two paths, one leading up to the vegetable fields, the other to the valley. This is the spot where elderly women stop for a break on the way home from their fields – a place where they can put down their laden baskets and rest. This usually takes place around 4 pm.

An overgrown edge of the hill was reshaped into a stepped topography, using sandstone as retaining walls. This established a direct connection to the reservoir 2.5 m above the main road level. A platform placed 20 cm above the reservoir allows people to sit and dip their feet. An extended part of the platform became the roof that covers the corner where the elderly women place their vegetable baskets. The new plumbing for the forgotten reservoir also provided a water supply for this extension, feeding a deep wooden sink for watermelon. The team recognised that watermelon, a fruit often to be shared, plays an important part in summer socialising. While the villagers are working in the field, this renewed and extended pond keeps the watermelon cool – a refreshing treat for the workers after a long day in the fields. It also operates as a drinking tap for passers-by.

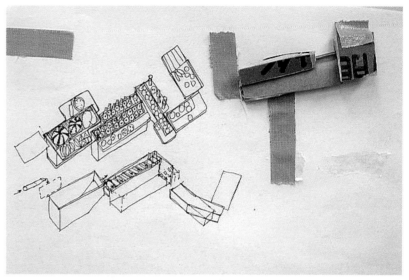

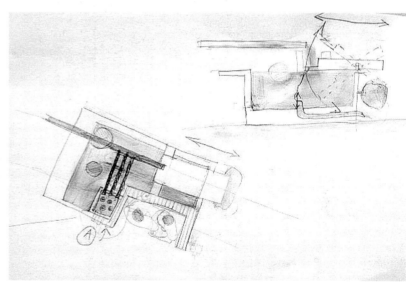

Study models and sketches of Watermelon Place, with extensions made the following year shown below.

Watermelon Place under construction.

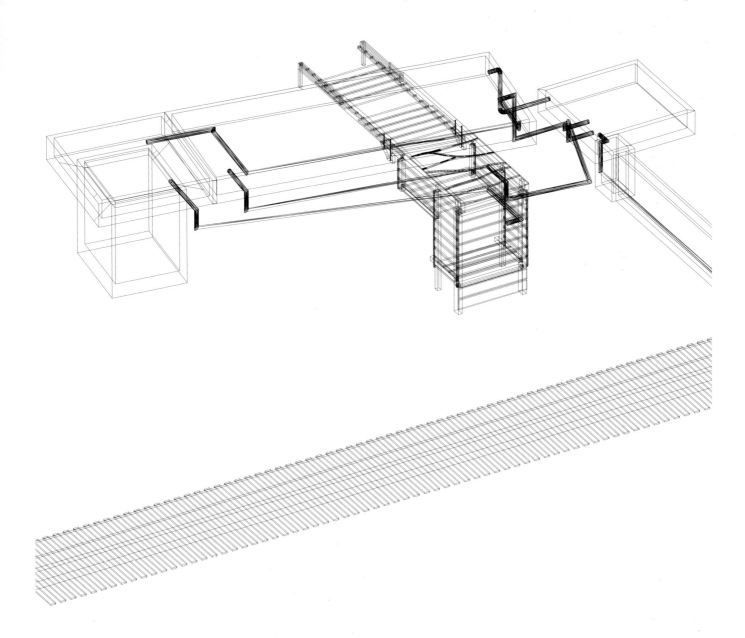

Exploded axonometric of Watermelon Place.

Watermelon Place in summer.

Additional Space

Edouard Cabey
Reem Charif
Maria Haralambidou
Maria Kamba
Christoph Klempt
Natalia Kokotos
Sam Liu
Hajime Muramatsu
Daisuke Nakaigawa
Kensuke Nishio
Louisa Fernanda
Sanchez
Sven Stainer
Yasushi Takahashi
Yoshino Takao
Stephanie Talbot
Daniel Titman

Shin Egashira

We began by identifying the absent volumes of winter snow as rooms in the summer landscape, individually mapping the volumes by placing our bodies within them. As we walked and uncovered these concealed spaces, our excursions became a modified game of hide-and-seek. A new hidden path was revealed.

Over the following two days we decided to extend this work into a collective effort. We created a place in the forest for all of us to sleep, a temporary tree-house overlooking the village from a distant hill.

Bamboo was the main construction material. Large amounts were donated from many back gardens, and harvested and gathered with the help of a villager and his white pickup truck. Long pieces of bamboo were used for the main structure, which was woven directly into the spaces between trees. Shorter and thinner stalks were split into various sizes to make lanterns, screens, rugs and seats. The flexibility of the bamboo – which varied according to the size of its section – determined the forms, surfaces and volumes of the spaces.

The main project was intended to facilitate places for 'additions' – activities or functions considered surplus to the usual pragmatic use of space as defined by production and efficiency.

The first team continued work on the bamboo lodging structure in the forest, before bringing it back to the school. Inserted into the interior of one of the classrooms, it formed a series of napping rooms (rooms within a room), with sleeping nests and screens woven in bamboo and supported at varying heights by added timber structures.

Star-Gazing Platform

After consulting the locals, this team learned that star-gazing was a popular activity for the parent and child playgroup. A few households had recently bought a telescope. The construction of a small-scale observatory became the theme of this project. We began with a search for a site with enough darkness at night, minimum interference from streetlights and houses, and maximum exposure to the horizon. The spot eventually chosen was in the playground at one of the highest parts of the village, where we felt closest to the sky.

A concrete foundation was laid to locate a telescope in precise alignment with the constellations. Timetables indicating the rotating cycle of the heavens were set in its surface.

The team also created a hinged structure that can rotate. It supports an elevated balcony for two: space for a child to sit safely at the front edge and a parent to stand behind.

Local Archive

This team began by visiting houses and mapping the objects kept in attics. Students inquired of the villagers, 'What do you keep in your additional space (slack space)? Is there something which has no practical use that you still hold on to because of its memory value?' Some of the things stored were implements that were no longer in use, such as a marking device for rice planting. Other discoveries included a *dakkokuki* (rice separator), wooden sleigh, bamboo basket, rice box, woven straw raincoat and snow boots.

The idea was to house the attic objects in a communal storage space, to be called the Local Archive. The site chosen was an existing yet forgotten loft space above the entrance to the gymnasium, into which all the school equipment had been thrown pell-mell. The creative work began by determining how to tidy it all up and relocate the objects. The cleaning work revealed original timber structures hidden beneath the dust and boarded up ceiling panels. A second phase of the archive's construction (a vertical extension) was proposed as a project to be passed on to a new team the following year.

Opposite: Star-Gazing Platform.

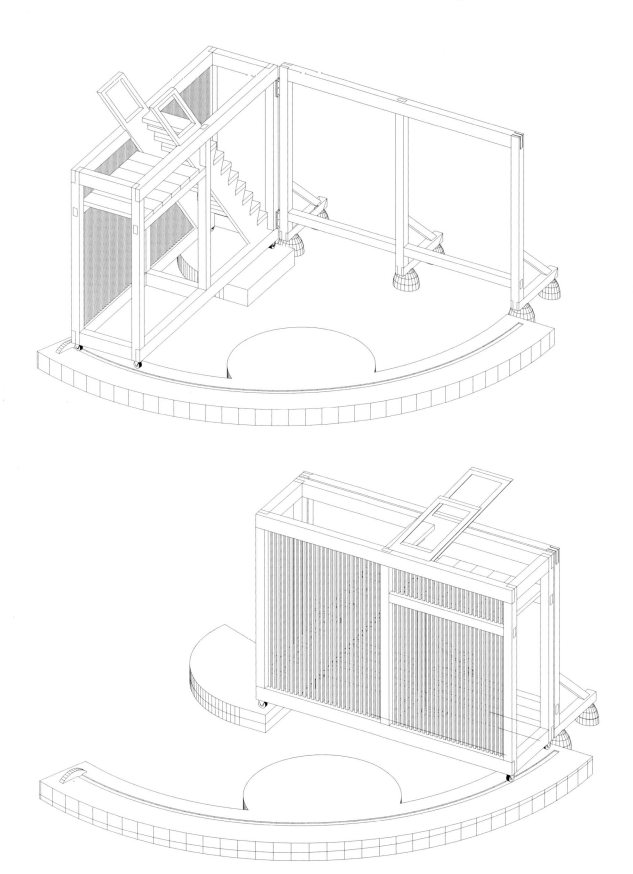

A temporary tree house made by harvesting bamboo
and weaving it into trees. Its life-span: two nights and
two days.

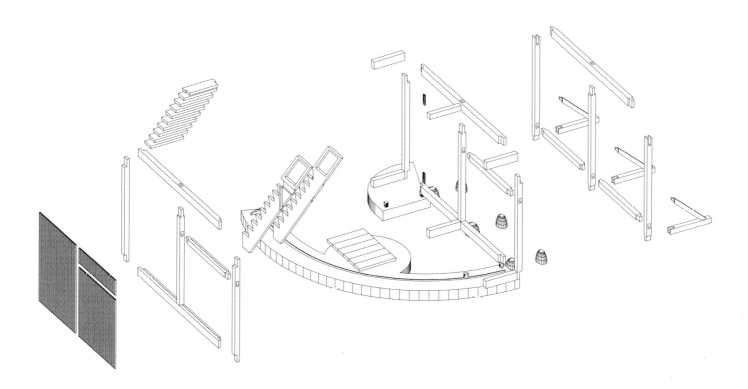

Star-Gazing Platform: The structure can be realigned along the radius of its concrete base in response to the earth's position in relation to the stars.

The view opposite bottom left is taken from the position of the Slow Window bench and shows the relation of the Star-Gazing Platform to the other structures in the park, including the Azumaya, Overpass and Moon Hill.

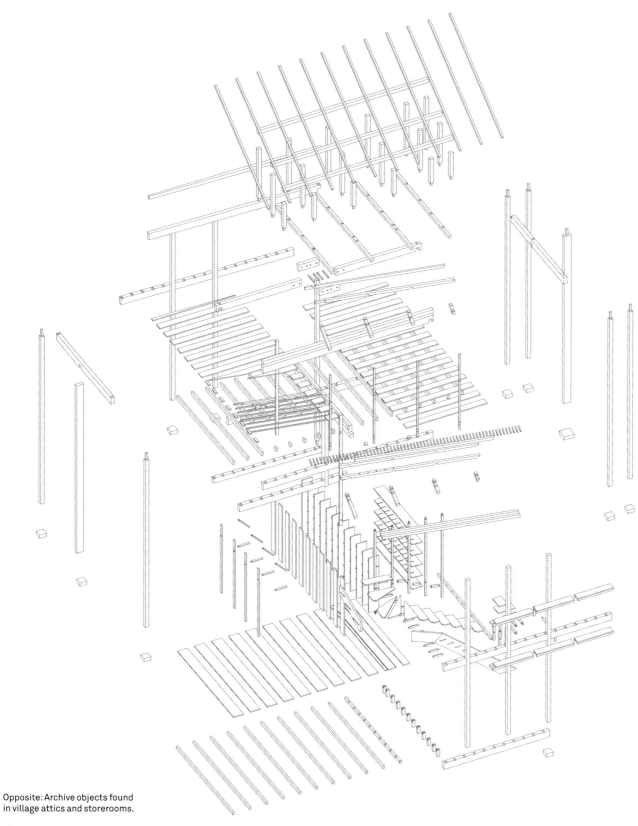

Opposite: Archive objects found
in village attics and storerooms.

Above: Local Archive exploded
axonometric.

Local Archive: A cut in the ceiling reveals the old structure and potential new storeroom. The new frame became a seating platform, with shelves as well as a ladder.

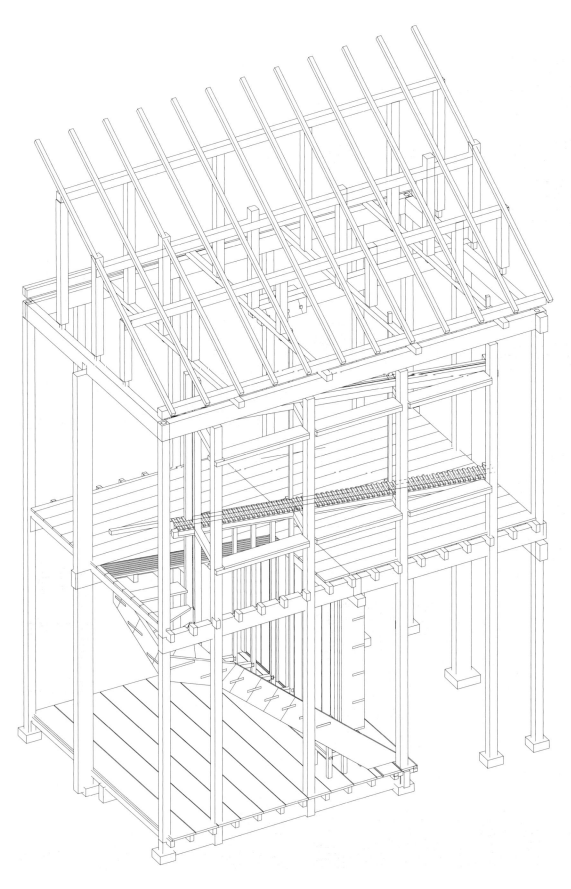

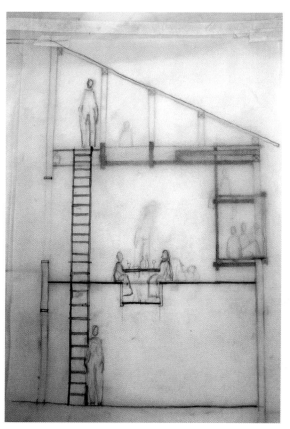

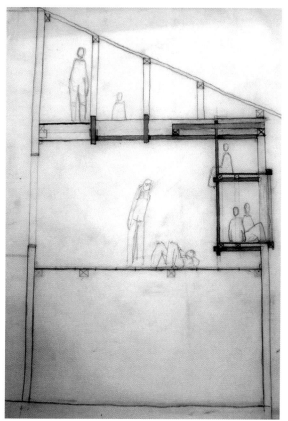

Clockwise from above: The geometry of the existing window frame was projected inward and its face rotated towards the Bus Stop, exposure of openattic; Local Archive works in progress.

Local Archive works in progress.

Temporary Structure

Michihiro Eguchi
Masanobu Eguchi
Haruo Eguchi

Joo-han Beak
Jake Choi
Laurent Duriaud
Hiroshi Eguchi
Ruth Garbus
Walter Guidry
Pedro Jervell
Nico Kafi
Kyoko Kobayashi
Haha Jze Yi Kuo
Sharron Lee
Yeuk-Yi Lee
Roberto Marsura
Rentaro Nishimura
Kensuke Nishio
In Joo Park
Catherine Annie Pease
Tatiana von Preussen
Adiam Sertzu
Mikolaj Szoska
Keita Tajima
May Tang
Mo Woon-yin Wong

Shin Egashira

The initial project was an experiment in staging narratives. Each team created its own scenario, sequence and spatial setup to accommodate a short story about two people meeting in various locations around the village. Six teams made six rooms for two. Six love stories related to six places.

Story 1: Hiroshi's childhood wish of helping a girl he admired climb a tree at the southern edge of the school grounds, so that they could watch the sunset together.

Story 2: On the road in front of the Water-melon Place, a man travelling from another village saves a girl's life on a very hot day by providing her with cool water and shade. An 'emergency love nest' tent structure was made from bamboo, rope and a bedsheet. A sprinkling of cold water was supplied via half-cut bamboo plumbing from the watermelon sink.

Story 3: A magic flying carpet with built-in picnic set can be hoisted off the road by the tree branch above it. It can also be used as a mantrap off the road.

Story 4: A natural shower booth made of bamboo extends to form a small waterfall at the lower edge of the village. It also works as a musical device in the landscape.

Story 5: An elderly man walks with his granddaughter along a familiar path paralleling the hidden course of an underground stream.

Story 6: A line connects a farmhouse in the village with a rice field situated across the valley. A young couple who wish to communicate with each other all through the day construct structures along the line. By drumming on the structures they communicate across the valley, signalling lunch break, afternoon tea and going-home time.

A Roof for 200

The main project of this year was to construct a temporary roof structure to house 200 people during the Maple Tree Festival. Our inspiration came from the Baito Festival that takes place on 15 January every year at the neighbouring village of Oshirakura, when the community builds a big igloo out of forestry thinnings and straw left over from the rice harvest. Our aim was to reinvent this winter festival, which has not been held in Koshirakura for several decades now.

The material we decided to use was 'surplus' timber – off-cuts from the timber industry and thinned wood from forest maintenance – joined with ropes. Our initial framework was formed of eight *nemagari* trunks, set out in the middle of the playground in line with the axis that runs from the Azumaya to the Slow Window and the Star-Gazing Platform. (*Nemagari* come from the lower parts of trees growing on slopes, and are bent from the weight of sliding snow in the winter. They have no commercial value.)

The secondary layer of the structure was composed of off-cut timber from sawmills, mostly end pieces of planks with incomplete rectangular sections, 2 to 5 cm thick. Applying the principle of gridshell structures, we bundled several off-cuts together with ropes and extended them into a series of strips 20 to 30 m long.

The final layer was the skin, which incorporated other types of off-cut timber from the mills, generally around 10 mm thick, 100-150 mm wide and between 600 and 1200 mm long. Local farmers often use these off-cuts as temporary shuttering for the rice field irrigation construction. The skin structure was first made into portable components then fixed in place on the secondary structure.

The other team joined in at this point to build a new suspended staircase from the main roof beams, penetrating across the existing timber ceilings and floor. This new staircase provides direct access from the entrance of the gym. A dinner party was held inside the dome on the eve of the festival. A gigantic hand, big red lips and four-metre-long chopsticks made for the costume contest were reused as lanterns inside the dome.

Opposite: Roof for 200.

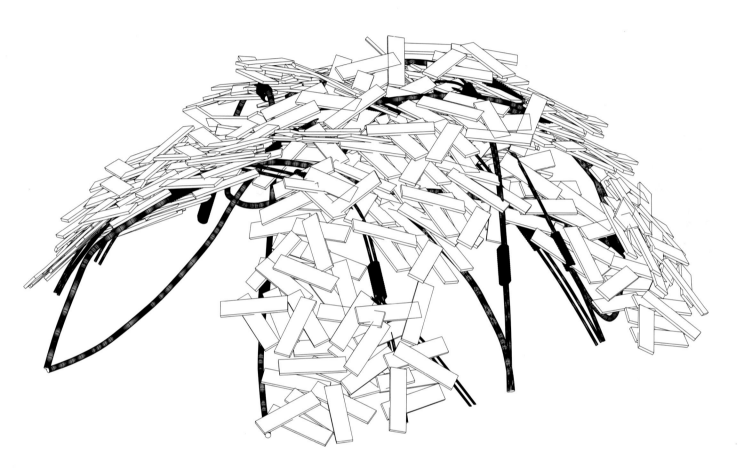

Story 1 left
Story 2 right

Story 3 left
Story 4 right

Story 5 left
Story 6 right

Roof for 200 construction process: *Nemagari* logs were used to set up an initial arch structure taking advantage of the bent and twisted geometry inherent in the timber. A further pile of timber off-cuts was donated by the local sawmill. Secondary components were woven and tied into the *nemagari* structure.

Roof for 200 under construction.

Rice rope was extensively used as a detail. As the loads increased, the ropes were
tensioned and the structure anchored to the ground.

The Momjihiki festival taking place in the structure.

Dismantling the roof.

The complete structure.

2003 Viewing Platform

Michihiro Eguchi
Masanobu Eguchi
Haruo Eguchi

Ivana Bocina
Hiroshi Eguchi
Maria Fernanda
Arrillaga
Ko Matoba
Francesca Muller
Takashi Nishibori
Kensuke Nishio
Akiharu Ogino
Adrian Priestman
Jenny-Elisa Schafer
Marisa Shaharia
Anna Shevel
Vikrant Tike
Takanao Todo
Lena Tutunjian
Ottilie Ventiroso
Zhi Xiong Chan
Yusura Zulkifi

Shin Egashira

At the end of the Maple Tree Festival the god returns to the sky, leaving behind the tree that carried him through the village. In the past the tree would be recycled as firewood for the winter. Nowadays, with less need for firewood, it tends to be chopped up for no particular purpose. Our objective – when we laid claim to the tree after the 2002 festival – was to reuse it as building material for the following year's workshop. We wanted to turn it into something solid and permanent: a horizontal gateway to the village, in the form of a viewing platform.

Our investigations began by selecting potential locations for the overlook. After the open presentation a site was chosen alongside the main road, halfway between the shrine and the school building, and at the edge of a steep drop along a 45-degree slope. A safety rail spans between two trees – a persimmon and a tall cedar. To the right is a small strip of cornfield. The teams outlined potential scenarios of how the platform could be used.
1   Local photographers visit regularly and use it as a tripod to shoot entire houses from above.
2   People stop and pick persimmons from the canopies above the platform. Sitting on the bench, they can view the autumn leaves while eating the seasonal fruit.
3   Grandparents sit at the edge of the platform, with their visiting grandchildren sitting in their laps. They share stories of the village and take family photos with the village in the background.
4   Weekend cyclists and motorists from the city stop to stretch their legs, taking off their boots/shoes at the edge of the platform.

Against the complex vertical topography of Koshirakura the level horizontal line of the gateway acquires a particular significance. Appearing as the most distinct (and artificial) landmark in the village, it refers to the notion of the palace as plateau. To begin, we worked with the topography of a maple tree, trying to understand it as a landscape, located against the flat floor surface of the gym. A series of sections were measured and made into jigs that compensated for the gap between the floor and the trunk. The jigs became integrated structures when they were lifted up and flipped over, supported by two ends of the tree as a beam; in this position, they became a series of 'floor joists' that illustrated the missing floor surface that now existed above the tree beam.

Two teams: one made a jig for the tree, the other made a jig for the site. Both began by clearing the surface of the tree/land to expose the topography hidden beneath the foliage, top soil or grass. Next they set up the projected planes above and below. The two procedures were similar, but executed at different scales and in different environments (at our workshop in the gym/at the gateway site).

As the construction of the jig gave way to the fabrication of the various elements of the gateway, the two teams split into four to take on separate tasks: 1 Foundation on site, 2 Main structure fabrication at the gym, 3 Flooring, built-in benches, picture frame, 4 Little look-out birdhouse for the corner of the platform.

Opposite: Viewing Platform.

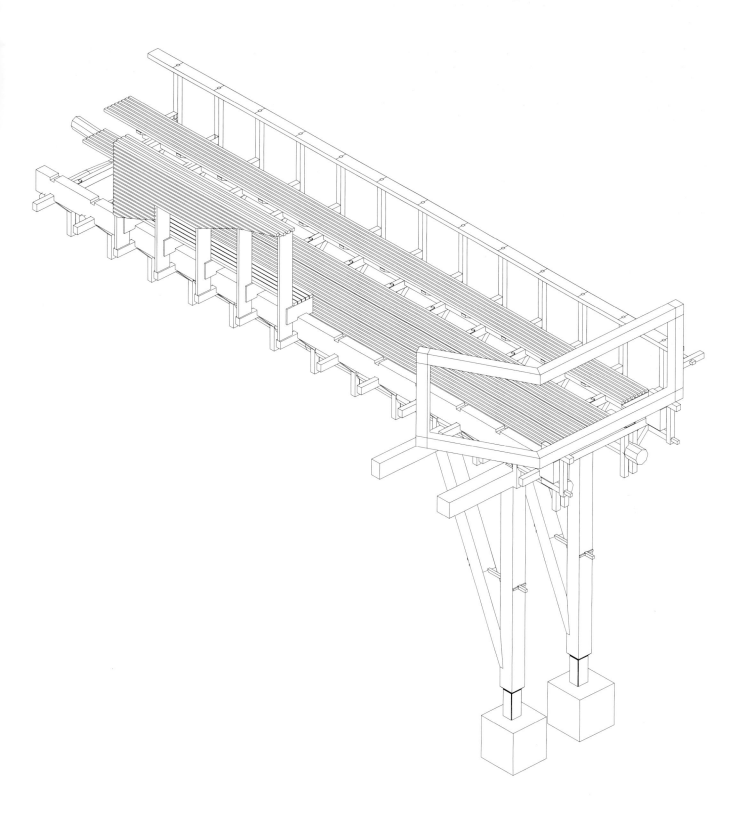

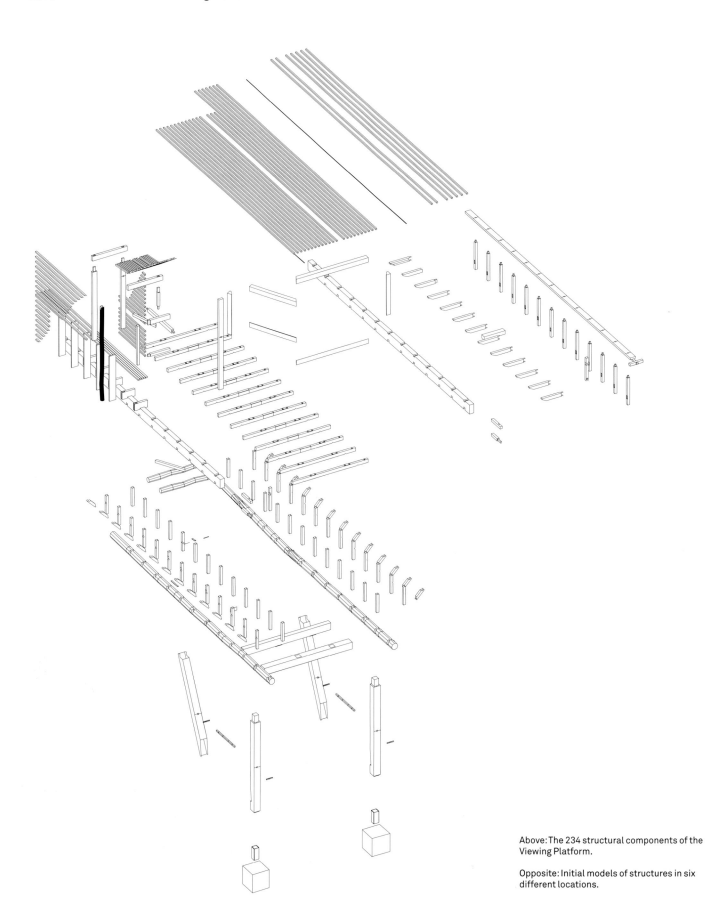

Above: The 234 structural components of the Viewing Platform.

Opposite: Initial models of structures in six different locations.

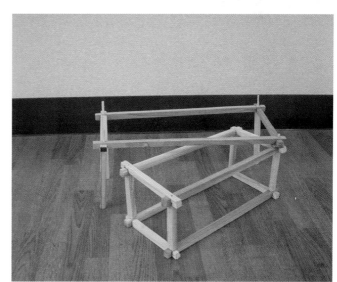

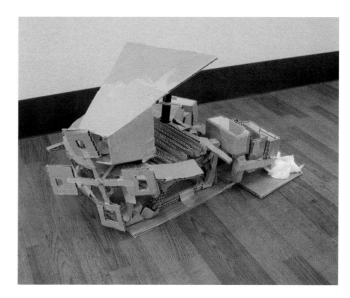

Measuring and making the jigs around the body of the maple tree. The jigs were replaced
by the platform structure and then flipped upside down so that eventually the maple logs
acted as main structural beams.

Corner view towards the village (above) and towards the road (below).

Michihiro Eguchi
Masanobu Eguchi
Haruo Eguchi

Xenia Adjoubei
Rubens Azevedo
Mei Chan
Panos Hadjichristofis
Rita Lee
Ryan Kwong Hung Li
Angela Lim
Sandra del Missier
Matthew Murphy
Maryam Pousti
Marike Schoonderbeek
Hyun-Young Sung
Chikako Takahashi
Shing On Evonne Tam
Nogol Zahabi

Shin Egashira

There are some folk stories that have been told for generations in Koshirakura. 'A Monkey Passed' is the story of a single father who once lived in the village with three daughters. A monkey offered to help him one harvest season, but demanded one of the man's daughters as his wife in return. When the father refused, he became very ill. To break the spell, the youngest daughter agreed to marry the monkey. But after they were married, she managed to trick him, sending him along the river before going back to her father.

With this and other tales in mind, we decided to devise narratives in response to four structures built in previous years – the Bus Shelter, Viewing Platform, Watermelon Place and Azumaya – to see whether rethinking spatial settings and functions could rekindle existing buildings.

The rules we set out to follow were:
1. Utilise elements of the existing landscape.
2. Write scripts and scenarios that could have taken place in the village.
3. Construct extra props to help stage the scenarios.

Three minutes of unedited footage were shot on four sites: in each case the cameras were carefully positioned to capture the structures as view sequences.

Team 1 set up a network of vistas starting from the Viewing Platform. A further series of window frames were constructed as props, placed apart but always visible from one another. These framed views are also linked by a series of existing paths around the village.

Team 2: The Bus Shelter in winter. Heavy snow slides off the roof intermittently. Inside, a couple are having an argument. The emotions of the built environment and of the couple are interlaced in the turmoil of the argument. As such, the building responds not only to natural climatic change but also to emotional climates. The couple become friends again when the bus shelter quietly opens up, a cool breeze clearing the air within. A little gift appears from under the *dogama* earth-seat.

Team 3: A man with an umbrella waits in front of the Bus Shelter. Across the road, by the Watermelon Place, stands an unfamiliar girl. Not far away, along the stepped retaining wall, sit a group of local women, chatting as they take a break on their way home from the fields. There is no sign of the bus, but the man seems unperturbed by its late arrival – or perhaps he is just unaware of the precise schedule. Instead, he seems to have found an excuse to approach the mysterious girl. The locals fall silent, realising what is about to happen. With a cup of cold spring water in her hand, the girl beckons. Unable to resist, the man draws closer. Then he hears a sound and turns around to see that the bus is about to leave without him. He looks back at the girl – to find she has disappeared. He runs after the bus, waving his umbrella in the air, but the last bus of the day has gone.

Team 4: A charming old lady with a basketful of tomatoes is said to appear in front of the Viewing Platform at certain times. One day a stranger sees her, and she gives him a tomato. The tomato grows and grows and starts rolling up the hill, towards the Azumaya.

Four short films became the basis for the making of 'Koshirakura Story'. We organised ourselves into two production teams: one for further filming and editing, the other for designing and building a local cinema screen.

Opposite: Cinema Screen.

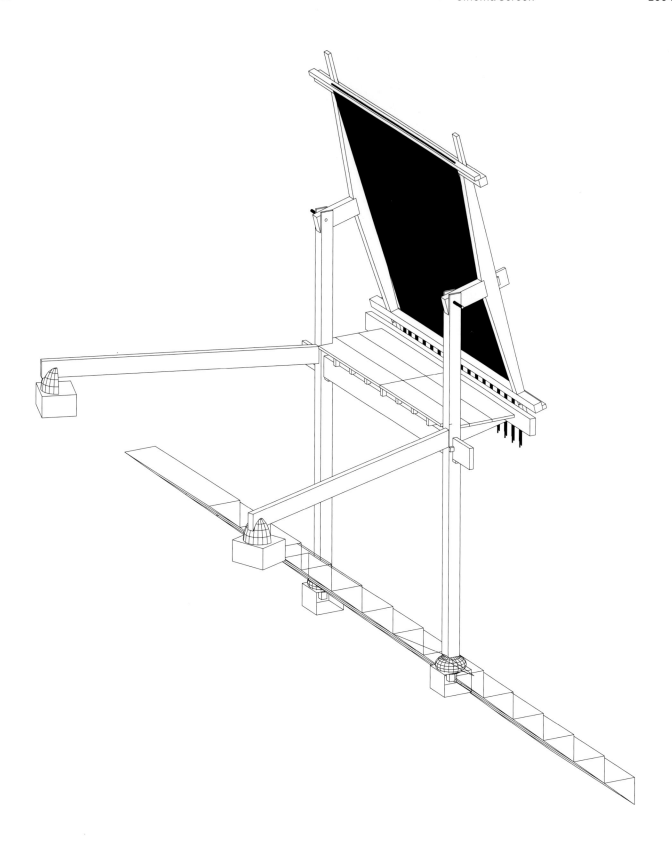

The space in front the shrine was chosen as the site for the cinema. The screen was aligned with the axis of the shrine. Projecting from the ground plane of the shrine, it extends over the stone steps that lead towards the village. The steps function as seats for the audience. The structure also becomes a new entry gate to the shrine.

Fabrics of different density were tested as projection screens, both for image reflection and movement in the wind. In the end we decided to use a great length of rope (3 km) stretched vertically between two wooden beams at 3 cm intervals. We discovered that the image could be seen from both sides of the screen, as the light reflected tangentially on the sides of each strand of rope and penetrated the gaps between. The structures were made with dry joints to allow easy disassembly and storage beneath the floor of the shrine during the off-season. Four anchoring points were marked by small pile-foundations surmounted with round stones.

The screen was adjustable vertically so that it could occasionally be used as a canopy over the main access to the shrine. A small shrine was also made to house a data projector. And a few seats were made from maple trunks. The production team shot additional clips in order to complete the story. Personal ads and promotions from local shops and petrol stands were also added. The film became a journey through the village, accompanied by Chikako Takahashi's narrations and combining invented stories with actual spaces. We explored new spatialities and ambiguities by means of the present topography and histories of Koshirakura.

Above: View of screen from bottom of the stone steps leading up to the shrine.

Opposite: Details of screen.

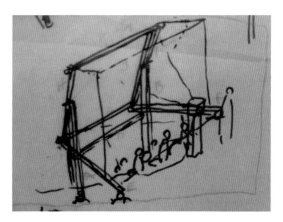
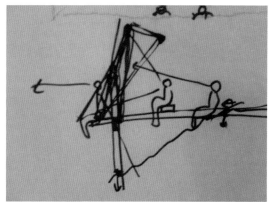

Clockwise from left: Sketches showing structures that enclose the temporary cinema space by taking advantage of the existing steps leading up to the shrine; dry joint models; process of weaving the rope screen; unrolling the screen; structural components, consisting of dry joints, simple tools and labour.

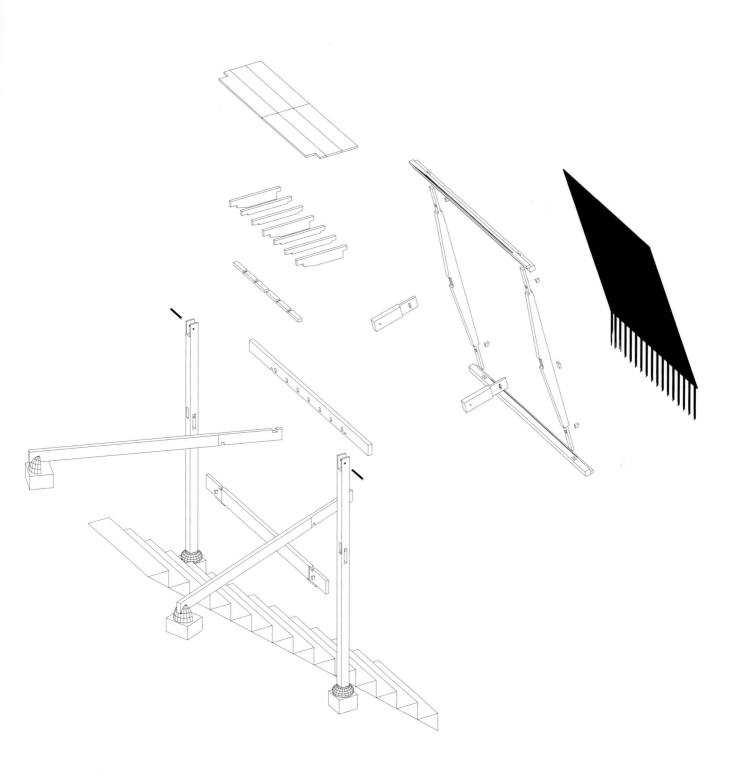

Night of cinema. The projection was imposed over the landscape scene viewed from the shrine. The images gradually emerged after sunset, as the darkness increased.

Noriko from the village shop advertising that week's special offers.

A small elevated platform in front of the screen allows live performances to be integrated with the film projection.

Opening credits of 'Koshirakura Story'.

Left and opposite: The temporary screen structure also serves as a gate to the shrine during the festival period.

Film series.

This page, above: In between the Bus Shelter and the Watermelon Place – the story of a man with an umbrella missing the last bus.
This page, right: On the road between the Viewing Platform and the Azumaya – a local lady with a basket of tomatoes.
Opposite, from above: In and out of the Bus Shelter – the everyday event of going to school; around the Azumaya – a restless house now occupied by seven different activities simultaneously; Inside the Bus Shelter – a couple argue and the structure opens.

Michihiro Eguchi
Masanobu Eguchi
Haruo Eguchi

Robert Buehler
Stephanie Anne
Edwards
Teppei Fujiwara
Mario Gottfried
Shireen Hamden
Taro Hosozawa
Seiji Kawai
Amandine Kestler
Sergey Kudryachev
Robert Luck
Sonaar Luthra
Veronica Manrique-
Charro
Espartacos Martinez
Noriyoshi Matsuzaki
Yoshihiro Miura
Shuji Mizukami
Orlando Oliver
Ill-sam Park
Krishan Pattni
Theo Petrides
Jesse Randzio
Marike Schoonderbeek
Daniel Ross Stevens
Yasushi Takahashi
Kenichi Tazawa
Shintaro Tsuruoka
Akira Uchida
Chao-Ching Wang
Masahiro Yamakita
Takeshi Yamakita

Hisashi Hara
Asao Tokoro

Shin Egashira

On 23 October 2004 the Niigata earthquake, registering seven on the Richter scale, shook the entire district of Uonuma. The aftershocks continued for several weeks, and were followed by unusually heavy snowfall in November. Koshirakura village was cut off from the neighbouring towns. The whole community had to be evacuated from their homes; they used the old school as a shelter, sharing the classrooms, the gym and the kitchen.

Once the electricity was restored, people became aware of the damage that had been inflicted on every house. And when the snow melted in early spring, the earthquake's real impact on the local infrastructure was revealed. Road surfaces were buckled and cracked. The distinctive patterns of terraced rice fields and irrigation systems were erased by landslides. A few buildings, the Slow Window and Star-Gazing Platform among them, had collapsed and were beyond repair. The earthquake loosened them from their foundations (they were set on packed earth rather than bedrock) and then the weight of the snow dragged them down.

Fortunately there were no fatalities in Koshirakura, though the disaster and its aftermath made the community – and especially the elderly– feel more vulnerable. Their longing for the arrival of summer was more acute than ever.

I visited Koshirakura in late March to meet with Kawanishi Town Council before it was officially wound up and absorbed into the City Council of Toukamachi. From April, Kawanishi town would be erased from the map of Japan. It was an emotional moment for everyone. Ironically the celebration of 10 years of the Kawanishi Landscape Workshop – founded on a promise made between Kawanishi Council, Koshirakura village and myself – was to coincide with the end of Kawanishi town. The concern in Koshirakura village was to ensure the continuity of the summer events, particularly the Maple Tree Festival. The villagers were looking forward to seeing the faces of the students who would be working with them that summer. The theme of the 2005 workshop was the making of life-expressions – manifest in built forms and objects as well as performances and celebrations.

The initial shorter project was to make film clips under the title, 'Koshirakura Story 2'. The key themes were love, loss and rediscovery.

Team 1's film clip is a romantic tale involving a man and an insect, which unfolds along the path between the 300-year-old cherry tree at the corner of the school and the small shrine in the centre of the village.

Team 2 related a journey through the village in search of a lost baseball. Shun, a local boy from the Katagiri family, and Marike, his friend from Holland, are playing in the gym. The story begins when Marike misses a catch and the two chase after the runaway ball. The ball is never found…

… Until Team 3 picks up the story. A stranger from the USA, camping in the wilds, finds the ball several days later at the lower edge of the village. It is finally returned to Shu on his bicycle.

The main project focused on the design and making of vehicles that could be used in celebrating the Maple Tree Festival. *Mikoshi* means a palanquin for the gods. It gave rise to the *omikoshi*, a portable shrine set upon four wooden beams that enable it to be carried from place to place. The Maple Tree Festival, however, is believed to preserve the concept of *mikoshi* in its original form, with a sacred tree being used as a vehicle for the gods.

But rather than emphasising gods and mythology, the vehicles we created were related to the activities of people and the recurring patterns of behaviour that unfold in response to the annual festival.

Opposite: Vehicle for play and safekeeping.

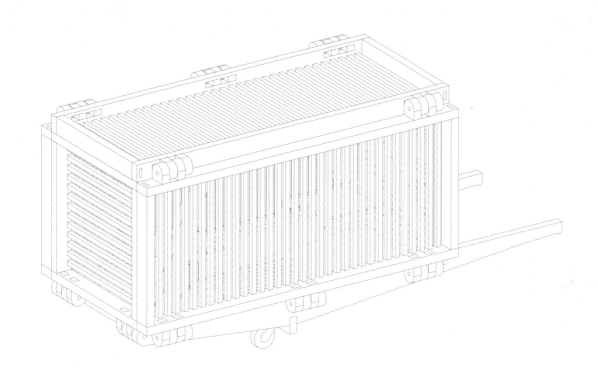

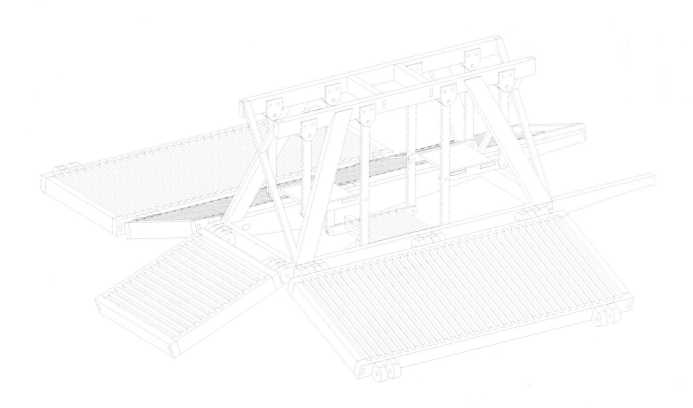

The construction process began by recycling the Slow Window and Star-Gazing Platform. They were disassembled into a series of parts which were then combined with new details in new structures. An unusable pile of timber was made into a big bonfire in the middle of the playground, which was lit by Masanobu San, the village chief for the year.

With the help of 19 sketch models we created a story-line associated with the Maple Tree Festival. At this stage, most participants only knew about the festival from photos and the stories told by students who had attended in previous years. This knowledge was often partial, and certain aspects and characteristics were interestingly exaggerated. The routines of singing, shouting, water pouring, playing and improvised games were translated into structural dimensions and mechanisms. Three teams were formed to design and construct three distinctive vehicles.

Team 1 made a vehicle for the expression of loud voices and pouring water. 3 mm-ply was cut in particular patterns and put together to form a megaphone. Combined with a wood box water-pumping device, it formed a two-wheeled water-pumping loud voice amplification vehicle that could also be used as a mobile seat for carrying a couple while showering them with voices and water.

Team 2 made a vehicle for play and safekeeping. Wood decking panels were folded around a swing set. The protective structure was designed to encourage children under six to participate in the festival activities while at the same time cradling them against the general boisterousness.

Team 3 made a palanquin for goddesses. During the festival the maple tree travels between houses to celebrate memorable events that have taken place that year, such as a birth or marriage, a special birthday, the extension of a house, or successes in business and studies. The mobile platform was originally conceived as a podium for speeches, for singing performances or for the celebratory kiss requested of a husband and wife. It was developed further to allow a group to sit together comfortably, elevated above a ground which was often awash with water from the celebrations. It was also put to good use as a shuttle vehicle for the elderly women of the village, who provide catering and other essential support for the festival.

The first two vehicles are folded and stored in the stage of the gym during the off-season. The third vehicle is used at two other sites during the year: under the cherry tree for the cherry celebration party in the spring, and as a small bridge at the bottom edge of the village. This last site has been used twice in past workshops for installations. Here the platform is located above the small waterfall, facing the terraced fields of rice which extend towards the horizon.

The festival was more crowded than in previous years, with additional participants from the neighbouring town, an English-learning group from Tachibana, architects from Tokyo and a volunteer engineering team sent by the Maeda Corporation. The cinema screen was re-erected at the shrine for the premiere of 'Koshirakura Story 2' on the eve of the festival (though a heavy downpour forced us to postpone the screening till the following night).

The new parade comprised the traditional *mikoshi*, followed by a line of three new vehicles carrying water, loud voices, wooden toys on wheels and people. There were more than enough participants to perform the additional festival rituals.

Opposite: The Slow Window and the Star-Gazing Platform after the earthquake and heavy snows of 2004. Recycling by sorting.

Overleaf: Small cardboard maquettes of Festival Vehicles.

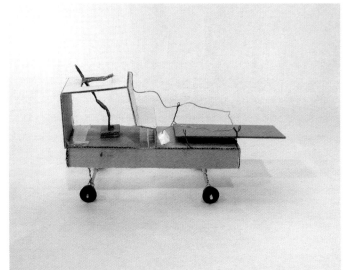

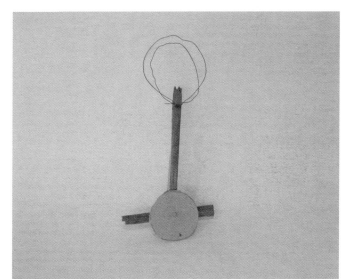
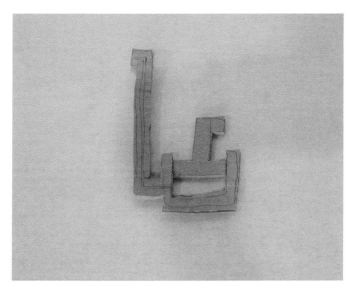

Vehicle for play and safekeeping: folding decking panels open to reveal a swingset (opposite), swing and hinge details (top row and bottom left).

Bottom right: 3 mm-ply patterns were stitched together to make a megaphone structure.

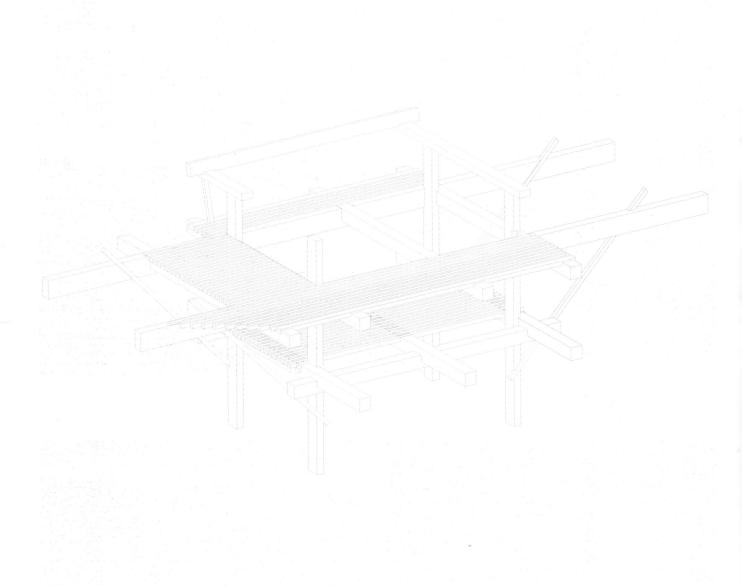

Opposite: Palanquin for goddesses. Above: Carrying the Maple Tree around the village. Below: After the festival the palanquin vehicle is reused as a platform over the small waterfall at the lower edge of Koshirakura.

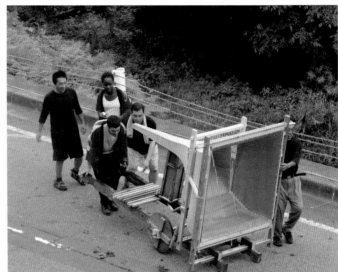

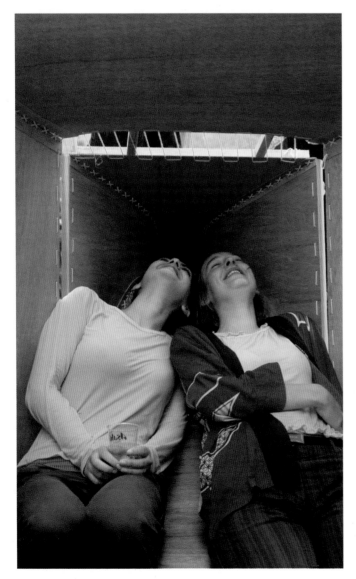

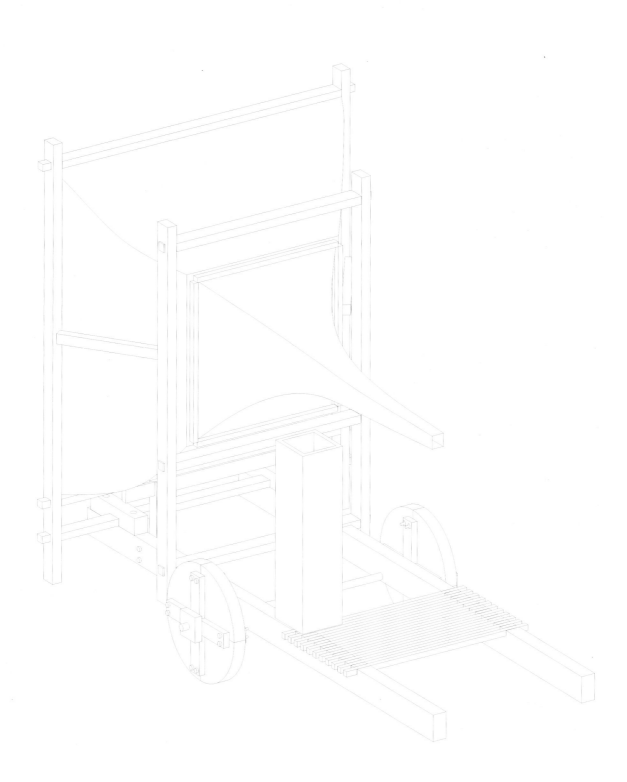

Above: Vehicle for the expression of loud voices and pumping water.

Opposite: Three vehicles in the Maple Tree Festival.

Extracts from Koshirakura Story 2.

1-7 Top of the hill to the bottom of the shrine steps – the love
story of a man and a beetle; 8-14 Starts from the school gym
and ends at the waterfall at the lower edge of the village – a
lost baseball and an American stranger; 15-17 Sheep dancing;
18 Shooting film by following a beetle.

Roof over the Shrine

Michihiro Eguchi
Masanobu Eguchi
Haruo Eguchi

Ivana Sehic
Jesse Sabatier
Isabel Pietri
Shintaro Tsuruoka
Jessica Reynolds
Jessie Turnbull
Joseph Bedford
Miriam B Waltz
Irene Sunwoo
Vincent Jiatian Gu
Kevin Lee Cash
Selina Bolton
Taneli Mansikamaki
Tessa Katz
Umberto Bellardi Ricci
Kyoko Ito
Marike Schoonderbeek
Chikako Takahashi
Aya Hidaka
Narimasa Kawamura
Hisaharu Tanida
Taro Hosokawa
Nobuyuki Tsuchida
Tetsuya Mishima

Documentary
Rubens Azevedo
Julian Löffler

Shin Egashira

Special Guests
Ken Mineta
Ei Mineta
Akira Uchida
Takeshi Yamakita
Nabashi Tomoko
Toshiro Hidaka
Takao Ishiwada
Satoru Taki

Reorganising the workshop after the closure of Kawanishi Town Hall became our agenda in autumn 2005, when Koshirakura as a village expressed its wish to continue the workshop.

The most obvious possibility was to approach the city government for funding. But we all agreed that however we organised the programme, it should continue to reinforce the combination of independence, openness and informality already inherent in the community. The idea of starting the new phase of the workshop by asking for greater government support didn't generate much excitement.

2006 was planned as a pilot year to test the new agenda and means of organisation. Funding came from a maintenance budget secured just before the closure of the Town Hall, supplemented by some savings from the previous year. There was an increased flow of vegetables, sake/beer and rice balls from the village houses to the school.

Our new programme addresses how to make the best use of a few houses and lots that lie abandoned for various reasons. The first phase will involve designing events and activities that rearrange these spaces, opening them up for communal use as small playgrounds – transitional slack spaces. Phase 2 calls for the construction of a new low-maintenance structure that will serve as a communal room (or house for visiting guests) run by the community.

Our chosen site contains an old house that has lain untouched since the earthquake reduced it to a heap of wood, straw and mud. It belongs to someone from outside the village who bought it as a weekend home a couple of years ago (but never managed to visit). As it took us a while to track down the owner, the programme was not ready to launch this summer. So we decided instead to contribute something practical to the most respected and used place in the village, the shrine.

The idea of a retracting roof over the shrine evolved as a response to the weather the previous year. Climate change has led to more unpredictable storms. A downpour on the eve of the 2005 festival meant that all the planned events had to be cancelled at the last minute. There was no film premiere, no dancing, no fireworks display. All the lantern decorations we had prepared were washed away.

Bamboo, rope and timber salvaged from the Slow Window and Star-Gazing Platform were used to make the main structure of the new roof and the retracting mechanisms (pulleys). Blue (the cheapest) and white (the most expensive) tarpaulin sheets were tailored into a striped pattern then stitched together and riveted. The edges were reinforced by the insertion of 6 mm-diameter plastic sticks commonly used as supports for vegetable-growing tunnels. Three canopies were hung from three trees to form big umbrellas. Integrated under the roof was another structure that extended the facilities of the Cinema Screen (made in 2004) by providing a pivoting bench seat and support for the projector. The structures are designed to be used once a year. On the eve of the 2006 festival there was no rain.

Opposite above: Preparations on the eve of the 2006 festival, showing the three canopies covering the entire site of the shrine. The umbrellas turned out to be parasols, as there was no sign of rain.

Opposite below: Pivoting bench before the film premiere.

Chapter 3   Diaries

I Do Not Teach Them How To Clean

Here in Niigata, sake (rice wine) is the unofficial tool for doing business. It makes everyone vulnerable and open to constructive discourse. Important decisions are often made over a drink: it aids the natural progression from formal to informal to an official happy ending. Once this ritual is shared, there is a sense of trust between us, and no written form of agreement is required. No matter how drunk we become, we all stand up at the end of the 'session' and congratulate the joint effort of the group, then collectively start tidying up the place up and clearing away glasses and dishes.

It was September 1996, a week after the first workshop in Koshirakura. We had used the former school building as our base during the three-week stay. It was in every way the model of an old elementary school, only minus the pupils and teachers. There was a heavy safe sitting in the middle of the staff room and a wall covered with framed certificates and portraits of previous school principals. We created a shower booth right next to the school kitchen, converted the staff room into a workshop and turned the classrooms into sleeping rooms. Everything seemed scaled down: chairs, desks, spoons and trays, chopsticks, even the toilets. It is amazing how much a person is able to adapt to different sizes. The last two days were spent cleaning. But in truth we could not really recall what the place was like before.

Sitting in a circle on the tatami floor of the Koshirakura local community hall were five officials from the Town Hall, around 20 locals and myself, not knowing quite what to expect.

'Thank you for coming to this meeting. This is our opportunity to reflect...' Mr Watanabe asked everyone to raise their glasses.

The chief of Koshirakura immediately began to speak: 'If you borrow things from others you have to return them even cleaner than before, especially if they belong to the community. This is Japan. We don't know how many years you've been away, but I believe this is commonsense. The school is our house, all of us grew up here and we still consider this our home, even though it no longer functions as a school.'

'I am very sorry that we made you feel the way you feel', I responded. 'We should be much more careful in how we use the place.'

'This is a matter of principle', the chief said as he turned towards the Town Hall officials. Then he looked at me: 'You teach architecture, right? Don't you teach how to use a building?'

After the school's closure the villagers had continued to maintain the building, taking on work that had formerly been the responsibility of the Ministry of Education. I realised this matter of principle was a kind of collective demonstration against the government which had closed the school. It also seemed that the villagers were still unclear about whether I had been sent by the government with an official agenda. Most of them thought we were a group of students from a carpentry school in London. Some thought they could find London in the USA. Others thought we were there to make beautiful watercolour paintings of their traditional houses and landscape.

I said: 'If you want to bring more people here from outside, even for a short visit, you should accept that there are bound to be cultural differences, for instance regarding the idea of cleanliness. Some of your children and grand-children returned here for the festival and I saw they were treated as special guests. I didn't see them help tidying up afterwards.'

'But you do not live here. My children visit every year, and you may not come back again.'

Mr Watanabe from the Town Hall stood up, straightened his back and spoke out: 'We haven't told you yet, because I wanted to make sure it was okay to suggest it, but we are hoping that Egashira-san will consider continuing the workshop next year, though we have not had confirmation from him yet.'

In fact Mr Watanabe had asked me on the last day of the workshop about the possibility of continuing. I told him that I would like to consider the idea very carefully, by reflecting on what we had or had not managed to do, in terms of the overall aims of providing educational opportunities and a local regeneration programme. But it seemed the most important thing was to show that we appreciated living in an environment where there was no distinction between how to live and how to work with the land and the buildings. So if cleaning was critical, then we should have learned how to do it much more carefully.

The chief said, 'You came and went and left us to clean up.' He was by now quite drunk.

I seized the chance to say something, instead of apologising again. 'I came here because I thought the government had shown an exceptional willingness to try something different to revitalise the local community and I wanted to contribute to it. I really appreciate the fact that this community did not treat us as guests, otherwise the whole thing might have ended up as a formal gesture.'

With the help of alcohol I added, 'If you prefer to maintain your school just as it is, then there is no room either for us or for the Town Hall to be a part of it. I would rather stay until tomorrow to give the school a very good polishing and then never see you again.'

Noriko-san said, 'But it was really nice to see the light on in the school in the evening and to hear noises coming from it. There is nothing more sad than the dark, quiet, empty school on the hill that can be seen from my kitchen window at night.'

Michi-san followed Haruo's wife's remark by saying, 'There were lots of broken slippers before and they were very old, needing to be replaced anyway, and we can't blame someone for having bigger feet than us.'

'You are absolutely right', Kazuo-san glanced at the chief and shot me a little grin, saying, 'It was very funny to see them using tiny chopsticks, and they weren't bad at all. Egashira-san didn't do so badly considering he had to take care of more than 20 children for three weeks and make sure they ate and worked and had fun.'

I said, 'I didn't come all the way from London with the students to teach them how to use chopsticks. Nor do I consider them as children – and I am not that old either.'

The rest of the conversation turned into a sort of drinking session, at the end of which we made a promise to continue not only for another year but for the next 10 years. I was left a little worried. Would the town be able to provide a budget? They had mentioned that the prefecture's plan very much depended on the presence of Mr Ogawa, who was returning to the central government the following year. Also the Town Hall could not officially consent to long-term funding for the programme, but instead had to review everything yearly. Yet here we all were making a rather optimistic plan for a 10-year commitment, with the help of a drinking ritual. Now when I think about how it happened, I wonder if it was some sort of conspiracy to test me.

The chief was half-asleep with sake, while Watanabe-san asked everyone to stand up for the final toast. The chief's wife told me that he is happier when the weather is fine. He hates the rain, as he's a roofing carpenter. Watanabe-san, Michi, Noriko, Kazuo and me, we are somehow connected.

End of Summer 2005

Sitting in a circle in the hall were Michi, Haruo, Masanobu-san and around 10 local people. This time there was no one from the Town Hall (Kawanishi Town had officially ceased to exist). I had gone expecting a casual drinking session after everything from the workshop had been cleared up and the participants had gone home.

We began with glass of beer. When we switched to sake Michi-san took out a set of papers and circulated them among us. On the cover sheet it said 'Village Workshop Support Committee'. Masanobu-san was listed as Official Representative, Michi as Secretary, then there were the names of about 25 people from the village. The paper expressed their wish to continue the workshop.

18.8 Initial meeting followed by cleaning
and organising space in the school

19.8 Kawanishi tour: Hoshina Residence,
Ueno Temple and other buildings

22-23.8 Home stay

20.8 Evening seminar with Seihan
Watanabe and Yasuhiro Hoshina

24.8 Evening seminar with Dr Tadahiko
Hibuchi and Nancy Findlay

19.8 Opening party with Koshirakura locals

22.8 Representation of the landscape

20-22.8 Project 1 Textural Reading

1.Geological sections

2.Maps of textures

3.Small hand-held textural objects

1996

Ken Mineta

I came to Koshirakura in 1996 having already worked with Shin on a series of workshops in an urban context. Most of these were concerned with the analysis and re-reading of contexts in relation to the complexities caused by rapid economic and political change. Koshirakura seemed to offer an interesting contrast and a different set of challenges: how to make changes by introducing something new into a place where the landscape and the architecture were inseparable – and determined by the unchangeable forces of nature rather than the economic and political benefits dispensed by the central authorities?

The workshop began with basic preparations for living and working in the former school. We must have appeared strange to the villagers, even comical, as we all squeezed into little chairs and desks originally made for children aged six to ten, facing the blackboard on the wall for our first presentation. But they seemed to accept us as oversize out-of-town elementary school kids, who were curious about all the things that were already familiar to them.

In the beginning, the main difficulties lay not in conducting our design research activities but in dealing with ordinary things such as food supply, telephone connections,

1.9 Maple Tree Festival   2.9 Open presentation at Town Hall

25.8 Joined by Nagaoka
University team

3.9 Joint party with Architectural Institute of Niigata,
seminar on Public Art with Fram Kitagawa

31.8 Final presentation:
landscape tour guided
by 20 chairs

4.9 Visit to Takayanagi Village

31.8 Project 2: Reading Chairs

10-18.9 Exhibition at
Yokohama Port Side Building

5.8 Searching for
ing places

26-31.8 Site
works: 20
locations

4-5.9 Site clearing

4-9.9 Documentation

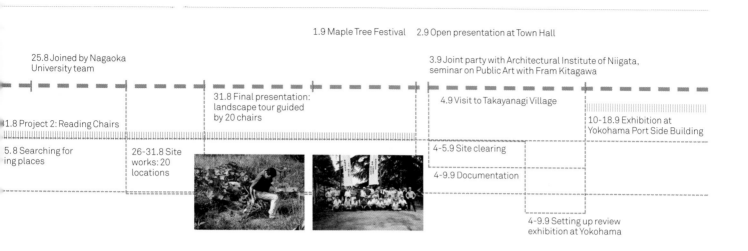

4-9.9 Setting up review
exhibition at Yokohama

cooking arrangements, insects, etc. We had quite a few late-night meetings with Shin to discuss how to survive within our modest budget.

Andreas Lang

Getting to Koshirakura

I arrived a few days late and made my own way to Koshirakura. I travelled by train, and the closer I got to the destination, the smaller and slower the trains became. It was midday, sunny and warm. I got off at a small station where I could see hills in the distance. Not being able to read Japanese, I got off at the wrong place.

Re-using the primary school

The workshop took place in a disused primary school located at the top end of the village. There were around 30 of us – a mix of AA and Japanese students – and we had the whole school to ourselves. Everything was designed for small children and therefore scaled down in size.

It was the workshop's first year, and there was an excitement about our presence in the village. Everyone was our host and seemed to enjoy the energy around the school, which was once again filled with noise, laughter and activity. Sport was one way to meet the locals, and the school gym became our playground.

The village extends along a winding road on the slopes of a hill. Many of the old timber structures have thatched roofs weighted with corrugated iron sheets.

A rural pragmatism is at work. Surrounding the village are rice fields; at its centre is a small shrine. Just over the top of the hill the road disappears into a tunnel, and the village seems to come to a sudden end.

Small-scale object

The first exercise was to make an object that related to the site. Everything around us seemed as soft as the earth, and held together by water. I took a solid egg-shaped clod of earth and hollowed it out before filling it with water. It was a strange object and I remember the bewildered looks when we presented it to a local audience.

Maple Tree Festival

After the selected maple tree was felled in the mountains (a ceremony called *matsuri*) I remember it turned up at the school swimming pool, which was half-filled with green water. The tree had ropes attached, and was pulled by the locals, who were all soaking wet. Suddenly a water fight broke out, and there was no escaping. Shin was thrown into the pool and the party began. Once we had calmed down enough we all started to pull the tree along the road through the village. Every time we passed any water, a fight erupted and the tree came to a halt. It was a hot August day and we soon got used to being soaking wet.

Several households had laid out carefully prepared snacks, and the mayhem would momentarily stop while we settled down for sake and something to eat.

Chair

Rumi and I invented a chair. At the edge of the rice field ran a small stream. The chair invited you to sit with your feet in the stream. We fixed a small vessel in the water, to support a straw from a rice plant. While you leant back and enjoyed the cool water at your feet, the water would move the vessel and the straw would gently tickle your face.

Itsuo Eguchi (villager)

Looking back, I had no idea what the workshop would bring when it first started. Everything seemed so curious to me, and when the students presented the projects to us for the first time, their unique points of view really amazed me. Now, I am always curious to find out what they will create next time. I still remember when I first invited the students to our home. They looked surprised to come into a traditional Japanese house. Since then, many students have come to stay with us over the years. I share so many memories with them: going to see fireworks in town on the back of a lorry driving along the motorway, having so much fun together decorating for the festival, getting soaked while dragging a maple tree on the festival day ... all of you touched our hearts with genuine emotions that made us feel so united. This tiny little village has been given such courage and hope by the young vitality from abroad. And I am glad that we all met.

20.8 Hoshina Residence design survey

18-19.8 Reading the landscape of
Koshirakura using 1996 maps

20-23.8 Project 1: Alternative Map
of Koshirakura, four teams

23.8 Open presentation at the gym.
Cherry-tree planting proposals
followed by volleyball tournament

24-27.8 Material salvage throughout town

24.8-8.9 Project 2: Bus shelter

25-26.8 Three propositions
in three locations

A. Colour

B. Sound

23-24.8
Documentation

C. Textures

D. Visual Field

Site 1: Steep corner east

Site 2: Water place

Site 3: Footpath junction

1997

Emu Masuyama

Villagers
A huge Indian guy, wearing a traditional farmer's hat, saying *konnichiwa* ('hello' in Japanese) to very little old lady on the street in the village. She must have been a bit scared at first....

The incident of the stripping girl
The figure of a scantily clad European woman, vigorously digging a hole in the Japanese countryside – a surreal image that she was quite unaware of. With the sun beating down on her back, she removed bits of her clothing to cool down. Old ladies carrying baskets paused as they passed by, bemused by this unusual sight.

Translations
Some men from the village visited with a big sake bottle in hand. I, a Japanese art student with no prior connection to the AA, tried to translate the rural Japanese dialect of Kawanishi for the international students and the English for the local villagers, but my translation just made things more confusing. In the end they seemed to have understood each other without my 'help'.

The first snow-melting place
A *yukigakoi* is an enclosing fence, detached from the main facade, that protects the house from the weight of the snow. In the winter the villagers slowly stack wooden boards (each about 300mm high) around their houses, keeping pace with the accumulation of snow. The houses have two entrances, one on the ground floor and another, for winter, on the first floor. As the snow piles up, the lower door is submerged. Every house has its own pond: in summer it houses a shoal of farmed carp, in winter it catches and melts the snow that falls from the roof.

The first snow-melting place is where snow melts faster than any other place, where you can see the ground first emerge after a long winter. We built a sliding picture bench at the bus stop to frame the view. The snow melts slowly, flowing into a pond; when the sound of flowing water is heard, spring has come.

Festival – thrown into water
Villagers and students dragged the maple tree along as a mobile shrine, visiting houses that had experienced a special event during the year – such as a marriage or a birth. At every pond along the way we were thrown into the water. Students, unit master, old man, child, young lady … it didn't matter who you were, everyone threw everyone into the water. We were all wet, it was total chaos. Whenever we stopped, huge amounts of sake, beer and food were consumed.

ropositions/making a
il components

30.8 Maple tree cutting
and carrying; fireworks
and karaoke dance night

31.8 Maple Tree
Festival

9.9 Official opening ceremony, bus arriving at
7pm, followed by farewell dance party at the gym

0.8 Maple Tree Festival decoration, preparations

Tenjinbayashi
sessions

5.9 Assembly of parts
in the gym

10-11.9 Two days of cleaning

27.8-8.9 Bus Shelter construction phase
Five teams

7-9.9 Woodshop team,
construction of secondary details

A. Clay-tablet firing

4.9 Foundation works at
sites 2 and 3

Kakishibu paint on the bus
shelter structure

B. Picture-framing bench

C. Stone foundation

6.9 Site team, main structure assembly,
roof beam erection ceremony

D. Timber joints

E. Snow-shuttering

7.9 Repositioning parts.

F. New detail construction team

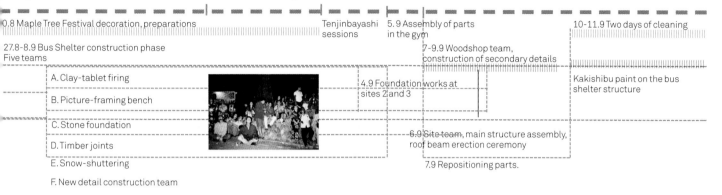

Takako Hasegawa

Three projects

Three projects to explore – an alternative
map of the place, objects, people and life;
a proposal for planting 30 cherry trees; and
a bus stop – the first in the history of the
village. The bus stop and the planting could
be seen as reinterpretations of the
particularity of the place, while the
mapping would help identify them.

The village

A winding uphill drive through rice fields to
Koshirakura amid a dense green, buzzing
with persistent cicadas, to a disused school
on top of the hill – our home for the next
three weeks. It is a picturesque small place
(a previous winner of the Most Beautiful
Japanese Village award) with only 48
homes and a largely elderly population. The
village is *kaso*, with no hope of recovering its
former population, but the villagers'
positive thinking sustains the place.

The magnificent cherry tree by the school
gate is 330 years old and the fourth largest
in Japan. A snaking, hilly street connects
scattered thatched roofs and many carp
farming ponds – previously rice fields. A
small shrine at the top of some stone steps
marks the centre of the community. There is
evidence here of heavy winter snow and of
earthquakes: *yukigakoi* and structural
columns sitting on big stones.

Stories with the villagers

Paying us a visit becomes a nightly routine
for many villagers, who bring endless
supplies of sake and singing. Tonight
Kitabori-san tells us a more intimate
history of the village. The local people are
the descendants of absconding samurais,
who used the place as a hideaway and lived
off the land. The village used to be
completely self-sufficient and the people
still know where to find the best water, sand
and clay for building walls; only stones are
carried from the Shinano riverbank.

Cherry tree planting

Our idea was to plant cherry trees at
people's favourite places, which were
mostly associated with childhood
memories ... a spot in the rice field, in the
school playground, by the small stream. The
mapping of the cherry planting suggested
alternative readings of the landscape:
the changing colours of the seasons, the
straight lines across the village that reveal
its topography and a map of memories and
stories. A major trunk road is planned to go
through the village in the future, some
beauty spots are likely to be lost – what can
we do to save them?

Bus stop

Katagiri-san's house is down the road from
the shrine. I liked its *tobukuro* (traditional
external sliding window shutter) and
thought we could use something like it in
the bus stop. I went in to ask about it and
ended up staying for hours, chatting over

18.8 Game construction in the gym

A. Play with wind

B. Play with water

C. Play with earth

Site works, planning

D. Play with sound

Toys project: material
sampling, making maquettes

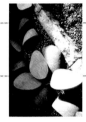

Project 1: Stay, observe and draw six locations

---

homemade plum juice with him and his wife. I returned to him for many more chats. At our next meeting about the bus stop we talked about the idea of a room as accumulated time and texture, the idea of anticipation – how to register the present that will become the past in the future. Eguchi-san told me the first snow-melting spot was the back garden of a small house that could be seen from halfway up the hill – a good spot for a bus stop. So it was decided: the summer stop would frame the view of the first snow-melting spot; the winter stop would be halfway down the hill, nearer the houses. The summer bus frame would slot into the winter bus hut when the season changed.

We mocked up the summer frame using plastic beer bottle containers – it looked really good. The concrete foundations required lots of digging. People stopped by for chats, wearing triangular straw hats and *jikatabi*, two-toed socks with soles, a style for field work. We went to collect clay in the open field, and by digging the earth found a good amount suitable for firing.

The winter hut was constructed in the gym, the summer frame in a classroom. The timber detail employs Japanese joinery. We designed and adjusted as we built. Needed to pour concrete foundation quickly, otherwise it wouldn't set in time. Textures moulded onto clay sheets – needed to dry them, ready for firing. In a rush. Celebration and night-time launch of bus stop. All excited, throwing candies from the roof of the winter stop.

1998

Kwan Guan Lee

Soba pillows

That first night I was kept awake until the wee hours. The soba pillow is supposed to let you sleep comfortably in the correct position for perfect spine alignment. My spine was perfectly aligned with the stiff wooden floor all right, but the pillow would not let me rest, so I tossed and turned. I later found out that the homonym of *soba* is *soda*, meaning 'near'. Near it was, to my mind, to my ear. I could not get used to the soba husks rustling in my ears. I think they rustled their way into my dreams eventually. This was my affair with the soba: 'Shi, sha, shi sha............'

The following days were packed with activities: visits to the homes of villagers, mappings and drawings, making and playing, walking and singing. The enchanted valley where Koshirakura sits welcomed us with outstretched arms and streams murmuring lyrical verses in rhythms akin to my night song: 'Shisha, shi, sha, shisha..........'

During the day it would get really hot, sometimes unbearably so. Tucked away in villagers' garden sheds were tools normally used in the winter. As we looked for them we listened to stories of Koshirakura covered in snow. Thoughts of winter came to soothe the sweltering heat.

Walking by the stream we saw Mr X, and offered him a cordial hello. 'Please come home with me. My wife will make you something to eat', he uttered in Japanese. So we followed him back to his house. As soon as we entered, his wife ushered us straight into the kitchen. 'Sit, sit, I will make you cold soba noodles'. It was like music to my ears, 'Shi, sha...Sshih sha.........'

Twenty minutes later, a bamboo dinner set arrived on the kitchen table with brownish grey soba noodles twirled into ten or twelve little balls and garnished with fine shreds of nori. 'Oh, wait, let me get some shiso leaves from the garden', said Mr X.

After a short briefing from Emu on the etiquette of soba eating, I carefully placed some spring onion, wasabi and red shiso in the soy-based dipping sauce. First the noodles in the sauce, and then, with a decidedly energetic slurp, it went down, so well, like spring transformed into a little ball of noodle rolled into my mouth, and a bucket of water emptied onto my head. It was refreshing.

'Shisa shi, shi sha, shi, sha........................'
Our project was to construct a playground for the village. Emu, Emiliano and I used the ground as a mould to cast three pieces of concrete furniture for the park. To finish the surface we rubbed soba husks over the exterior while the concrete was still wet. If you run your palm along these pieces of furniture and place you ear near to the surface, you can hear the whispers, 'shi, sha, shhi, shhi, sha, shi, sha......................'

23.8 Grass-cutting party   25.8 Lecture by Dr Kurono   26.8 On-site drawing presentations

30-31.8 Maple
Tree Festival

3.9 Presentation to the
council on site

6.9 Cleaning and
Farewell party

24.8 Hoshina Residence survey

28-29.8 Home stay

5.9 Playground phase 1:
public opening

26-30.8 Festival decoration

27.8 Cutting trenches

AB	Slow Window
AC	Wet Projection
AD	Dragonfly Sticks
BC	Harmonious Local Materials
BD	Quiet Stone
CD	Clear Viewing Platform
ABD	Ground works

26-27.8 Gathering sandstones from
Shinano River

1.9 Timber structure on site

25.8 Foundation works

14.8 General meeting

15.8 Bon Festival dancing.
International cooking session

20.8 Home stay

25.8 Ueno Autumn Festival

16.8 Playground review

18.8 Hoshina Residence/
Ueno temple survey

22.8 Volleyball match: workshop
v the village

Slow Window
Wet Projection

23-28.8 Slow Window construction on site

24-28.8 Landscaping

Azumaya/Summer Pavilion

20.8 Foundation works

23-28.8 Azumaya framework construction

Groundworks

16-21.8 Pinhole camera documentary

22.8 Pinup presentation in gym
Azumaya sliding furniture construction

Food

We were a group of 20 students from all over the world. Cooking for each other was a real task, and most of the time the results were a disaster. Some in the group were appreciably talented in the kitchen, but most had never cooked for so many people before. In all, it was fun, the cooking part more than the eating part. The villagers were intrigued by the different cuisines we rustled up for ourselves and decided to hold a huge potluck party with us in the school hall. The whole village participated and everyone prepared something from their country of origin. We ate and drank the entire night.

Wan Sophopanich

Rain

'It doesn't really rain here in the summer, this is going to stop soon', or so we were told; but in 1998 the Koshirakura workshop seemed dominated by rain, moving from moments waiting for it to stop, to being soaked through again.

A snow-keeper for the playing field, somewhere to cool beer and provide shade

To make the cooling mud wall, we went up to the playground after lunch to collect some earth for testing back at the school. The ground was particularly hard and the going was slow. Soon the villagers were showing up to play their daily game of croquet. Someone came over to see what we were doing, and simply laughed out loud

when we told him our problem; the playground was a result of a cut in the mountain to create level ground – what we thought was top soil was in fact the compressed earth in the middle of the mountain.

With the rain pouring down, we dug our foundations. At night there was salsa dancing in the gym, glasses constantly refilled with sake, a volleyball match with the villagers. When morning came we returned to the dug-outs, scooped out the rainwater that had filled the holes from the previous day's work and started the process all over again

It continued to rain, but the columns were up and the mud wall well on its way. The rain broke for a while, just long enough for the canopy to be completed.

Toy

From raw materials we collected in the village, some ropes and small ceramic wheels, we created what became known as the 'dog'. The dog-walking activity was often sabotaged by other toy-makers getting in the way – wheels dragging on the floor followed by jumping feet and silence.

Matsuri

More glasses of sake before setting off into the mountain to cut the maple tree for the festival. Water splashing, tree dragging, food, beer and sake.

Hiroshi Eguchi (villager)

My first encounter with the landscape workshop was in its fifth summer. I was back home from Tokyo trying to recover from city life. During what was for me an emotionally difficult time, I heard that foreign students were doing carpentry at Koshirakura School. Curiosity took me there to have a look: there in front of me was something I've never experienced before in my life.

I was greeted with 'Hello, how are you?' with a strange accent. Not knowing how to respond, I just returned an awkward smile. I still remember standing there just watching what was going on, until one of the English students came up to me, waving his hand as if to say 'come and help me!' His name was Inigo Minns, the first foreign person I had ever spoken to. Gradually we became friends, managing to communicate with gestures and actions. I found myself really enjoying the workshop, soothed by the open-hearted atmosphere. Eventually I realised that I had forgotten about my own depression. Since then, I have enjoyed taking part in the workshop every summer. If I hadn't had a chance to participate in the workshop projects, I would never have known the joy of making things, the happiness of accomplishment after going through tough challenges. People in the Japanese countryside who have been leading monotonous lives are now experiencing foreign cultures and establishing strong ties. Like a kindling

28.8 Interim presentation
on site

29.8 Grass-cutting day

4-5.9 Maple Tree Festival

28.8-3.9 Festival decoration

29.8-2.9 Moon Hill, Overpass and
landscape finishing

29.8-2.9 Moon Hill, Overpass and landscape finishing

29.8-4.9 Azumaya, Slow Window final construction

28.8 Interim presentation on site

29.8-4.9 Azumaya, Slow Window
final construction

flame growing into a large fire, a number of small projects built over the years have fostered many lasting memories. Not only the physical architecture, but the human architecture as relationships are formed. It's wonderful to be able to stand on the structures of our own creation, to have a view of the village from angles we never knew before. The landscape workshop has made all these things possible. I believe that the experiences here have also enabled the AA students to open their eyes to new ways of seeing.

1999

Bibiana Zapf

Sirens and insects
The siren goes off at 6.00 am to wake people up, at noon to mark the lunch break, and at 6.00 pm to call everyone back from the rice fields. Although everyone in the village has a watch now, and hardly anyone works in the rice fields anymore, the siren still reminds people of those key moments in the day.

The insects are on average palm-size and make an incredibly loud noise when they fly; they are absolutely everywhere; I can hardly sleep at night for fear of them finding a new home in my sleeping bag. It is almost a relief to be woken at 6.00 am by the siren.

Pinhole camera
I load the small box with paper and start with a two-minute exposure: the result is a blank photograph. By the following day we have worked out that the optimum exposure for a coke can camera is about 45 minutes. Larger cameras the size of a wine carton require several hours of exposure. We hold onto all the rubbish – it all provides possibilities for cameras. And we stop getting upset when people don't answer us – they are posing for that half-moon-shaped, taped-up piece of cardboard on the table in front of them.

Homestay
Michi-san and Kazu-san's house was largely modern, with glimpses of traditional elements and a workshop in the back for manufacturing small car-parts. Invited to be part of their family for the 24-hour 'homestay', we sat around the table for dinner, with Michi-san's elderly father communicating through a variety of visual vocabulary, little drawings and all sorts of photographs. Kazu-san invites us upstairs after dinner, gently wrapping us in layers of her best kimonos; returning downstairs, we add another image to our newfound visual vocabulary: a photographic portrait of the new 'family' standing together seriously, all clad in traditional clothes. Adopting us for the length of our stay, our family provide us with food and tools during our late hours of construction, and traditional family robes for the *matsuri*.

5.9 Playground phase 2 opening ceremony

6-7.9 Cleaning   7.9 Farewell party

8.9 Playground official opening

Phoebe Dakin

Pinhole cameras
pinhole views of the village
the body and the land
with reflections of the sky on flooded rice
fields

The fisherman-dance next to temple
a time to dance
dimly lit kimonos delicately stepping
forward back back
with defined arm movements around
eloquently faded lanterns
to rhythmically recorded sounds.

Azumaya
1 Material
wood and string. measuring.
displaced earth. digging.
big stones. placing.
sand and gravel. filling.
flattened. compressing.
steel reinforcement
into ground. hammering.
tied together. binding.

The carpenter's shed
Toryo-san wears an avaitor's cap and big
glasses, a *tabi* and pulled up socks
the intoxicating smell of wood and trees
touch wood
plane wood
mark and cut
a thin-ply template of the structure on his
musty attic floor is our introduction to the
azumaya.

2 Construction
a 12-hour carpenter's day.
morning exercises to stretch: in my mind a
little overambitious for 7.30 am.
marking and cutting each element of the
structure.
three rows of white poles along the field at
dusk; silhouettes of dragonflies playing
against the fading light.
earth forms in concrete and mesh.
water channelled to allow bridging.
delicate structures of moving roofs.

wooden elements transferred to site.
evening work by electric lamps;
six stage sets with dramatic lighting and
activities.
noise of human and machine and earth.

assembling of the elements.
site alterations and circular saws.
a necessary volleyball match: workshop v
Koshirakura, once again we lost.
perhaps slightly unfair having been drained
of energy all week.
jovial drinking spirits and singing of TJB
with an honourable aid from the village to
help erect the structures by dawn.
a triumphant skeleton and one hour's
sleep.

Homestay
an invitation for three to the Eguchi
household; Haruo-san and Noriko-san,
their sons and families and numerous
cluttered belongings dispelling any belief
in Japanese minimalism.

2000

14.8 Workshop begins	15.8 BBQ and karaoke contest at Azumaya		19-20.8 Home stay

14.8 Graveyard visit/Bon dancing

15-18.8 Mapping local networks/
meeting places

1. Local timelines

18.8 Group presentations to the village

18.8 Maple tree selection committee tour

18.8 Group presentations to the village

A. Slow Window extension

2. Water networks

B. Bus Stop extension

19.8-1.9 Extension projects
in three sites

C. Watermelon Place

3. Shared Spaces

---

all under a large blue roof. surrounded by carp, fresh vegetables and views to the hills. an evening banquet of delicacies; sake and beer with unending generosity and smiles. an insight into the history of koshirakura and ancient black-and-white photos of stiffly dressed relatives in exotic landscapes.
dark corridors, still more screens of privacy unending fodder for a child's imagination.

a morning trip to their rice field. a truck ride away. through terraced valleys and up forested hills.
the sun shining on us.
why should he desire to work anywhere else?
the sky, mountains, rice and water.

a kitchen goodbye:
soba and tempura sitting in the heart of their house and celebrating a way of life.
sent home on a full stomach to watermelon juice, joinery designing and a task to learn the local song.

i have no memory of birdsong.
cicadas sound incessantly to a happy heart.
'i have no need for a house key', i am told, 'and you are welcome any time.'

2000

Maria Cheung

Extension of bus shelter: oven seat

The seed of the idea to create an oven seat in the bus shelter was sown during visits to local houses. It was on one particular visit, to Heide's elderly mother, that our imagination was captured. As we sat in the living room drinking tea, with electric fans and open windows cooling us in the intense summer heat, she spoke of ways of keeping warm in the freezing winters. She showed us the traditional stove in the square, sunken central part of the room, heated by *rentans* – cylindrical blocks of coal with air holes to improve burning. One rentan (about the size of a one-and-a-half-litre tin of paint) would provide enough heat to warm the room for an evening as well as cook a pot of stew – though she rarely did this, as most of her cooking was carried out in the kitchen. She then showed us a *dogama* – a kind of clay oven that is now rare (few people still know how to make them, and gas ovens and microwaves have long made them redundant). Inspired by what we had seen, we knew that our project would somehow incorporate elements of heating and cooking.

One of the best-loved pieces created by the workshop is the local bus shelter, made primarily from timber and corrugated plastic using traditional local carpentry

techniques and ideas from vernacular architecture. Built hard up against the road and backing onto the steep slope that overlooks the lower, more populated valley, it was designed to be used throughout the year. It provides shade from the intense summer sun and shelter from the rain, and can be shuttered up, leaving only a small opening, in harsh winters when three metres of snow can settle. In the morning the local children await the arrival of the school bus, accompanied by their grandparents. In the afternoon the grandparents await its return on their own. So the bus shelter is not just a place for waiting; it is also for resting and meeting.

Through further conversations with the villagers we discovered that the number of children of school age had increased since the shelter's completion in 1997. This meant there was the need for an extension, particularly for the winter months, when there was no longer enough space for all the children and their grandparents to wait inside.

During our investigations into local building materials and practices, we met the father of Katari-san, one of the few people who still knew how to make a *dogama*: this was an opportunity to learn a traditional construction technique. The following days were spent working together with people from the village to gather materials, learn how to make a *dogama*, and investigate how it could be used in construction. We collected truckloads of red sticky soil which is used locally for

21.8 Sakurai Toryo seminar on mud-wall construction
20.8 Grass-cutting day with the elderly group
24.8 Interim presentation on site
2-3.9 Maple Tree Festival

21.8-1.9 Festival decoration
24-26.8 Collecting local stones, mud and clay

27.8 Wood planing at Igawa's sawmill

planting rice seedlings, sandy red earth from a local building site and straw from the previous harvest. The school driveway turned into a large outdoor kitchen for our experiments. Similar to making a cake, the soil was sieved through fine woven baskets to remove unwanted stone and sand. The straw was beaten to break down the fibres – initially we used small wooden hammers, but later discovered that driving over bundles of hay with an eight-person van produced the same result with a little less effort. Moistened with water, manageable mounds of the ingredients were mixed together by stamping our feet in a large makeshift mixing bowl (timber joists and a tarpaulin sheet). Once the air was stamped out of the mixture, it was divided up to make small volcanoes that were filled with water and left to ferment.

A *dogama's* structural integrity is informed by its shape – a vertically stretched dome which doesn't need to bear any load and so has no need for reinforcement. However, we were trying to create a dogoma with a side chamber – a heated seating element – so some form of structural support was necessary. We experimented with mesh, but in the end decided that we should use the Japanese carpentry skills that we had learnt. Whilst our ingredients were fermenting, we refined the design by building mock-ups of the oven seat using timber and block work, and tested the effectiveness and viability of using rentans as the heat source, as well as developing the design of the bus shelter extension.

The location of the existing shelter – hard up against the road and very close to a timber electricity pylon – meant that our intervention would have to extend the shelter away from the road, over the steep banks of the valley below. A simple timber structure increased the depth of the bus shelter, which allowed the arrangement of face-to-face seating, as opposed to the previous linear layout. We had envisaged a cantilevering extension that would have put too much stress on the existing structure, so in an effort to continue the spirit of using local materials, we 'borrowed' three very large rocks from the shores of the local Shinano River which became the vertical support and foundation of our extension. Fuelled by fruit, vegetables, sake and encouragement from the villagers, we worked through the days and nights to construct the extension, only taking intermittent breaks to join in local feasts, karaoke and haiku competitions and dances. Our deadline for completion was *matsuri* and the Maple Tree Festival.

Reem Charif

Running water
Quiet village with the sun beating down. Everyone was indoors getting on with things – except for some old ladies with their handmade wicker baskets, collecting vegetables from the nearby fields. The sound of running water came from all directions, like an open tap. Fresh water, ready to drink. Any house was happy to offer, no need to ask, just help yourself. Small ponds or metal sinks – supplied with small mugs or soupspoons – collected the water that slowly flowed from not quite closed taps. The containers were laden with vegetables, fruit, beer and lots of delicious-looking things, all cooling under the flowing water. Watermelons took most of the space, bobbing up and down as we interrupted the water flow to drink. The overflow was channelled into secondary concrete ponds in which orange and white carp darted around, occasionally tasting the air above.

The old ladies of Koshirakura
We sat in the shade, as we had the day before, watching the old lady cutting the watermelon into thin triangular slices; she gestured that we should eat them by hand, 'more delicious that way'; she offered new pieces just before the last were finished. No one was saying much as we sit there smiling, eating the watermelon, listening to the sound of the knife slicing through the sweet pink, the forgettable white and the resistant green and then the sharp tap

6.9 Opening of extensions

3.9 Baseball match: workshop v the village

6.9 Cleaning and farewell party

7-9.9 Takakura gym cleaning

5.9 Open presentation of Slow Window

4.9 Open presentation of Bus Stop and Watermelon Place

15.8 Village BBQ under the cherry tree
16.8 Bon Festival dance at the shrine   19.8 Fieldworks/soba planting

23.8 Dinner party at the storage site
24-25.8 Homestay

21.8 A night in the woods

19-21.8 Project 2: Lodging in the woods –
a treehouse for 15

23-24.8 Cleaning the sites

16-18.8 Project 1: Seating places –
15 locations

21.8-3.9 Project 3: Slack space

A. Slow Window observation
platform diversion

B. Room for having a nap
(classroom conversion).

C. Star-Gazing Platform

D. Archive as communal storage

E. Communal sink for the
Watermelon Place

24.8 On-site

when the metal met the wood. Old ladies with wicker baskets on their backs and straw hats on their heads appeared at midday and sometimes in the afternoons; they travelled between the smaller fields collecting their vegetables and fruit. They stopped and rested at the forgotten pond on the way down to the main road, resting at its edge, fetching water from the enclosed part of the pond with the awkwardly sized and placed squeaky door, almost disappearing into it as they reached down to fetch some fresh water.

Vegetables on the doorstep, watermelons near the kitchen, aubergines near the main door, tomatoes by the window. The old ladies must have dropped by. They would never announce their arrival but would shyly place their gifts all over the place – like a treasure hunt for us to find.

Watermelon Place
(also known as the watermelon event)
A point of gathering for the old ladies on their travels.
A space to formalise the happy social effects of watermelons.
A platform collecting the practices discovered about the village and re-arranging them back in a two-storey event space.
A freshwater tap sheltered under a platform that allowed chinks of light.
A hill carved out with concrete casts that mimicked the shape of the body.
A small tailored wooden box for cooling the vegetables.

Climbed through an opening in the roof, past the tap, up into the deck.
The roof as platform connecting the two layers and spanning from the edge of the pond water out into the village.
A raised view of the village.
A deck to lie on and look at the sky.
An edge to sit and chat with your feet in the water.
A circular opening, for many to sit around, waiting for the watermelon to get cold.
A place where the watermelon would dance again.
A chopping board to call old friends, sounding loudly when the meeting had begun.

Grass-cutting
A collective event of clearing the school grounds. The elder generation of the village arrived with farming tools. They demonstrated with gestures and smiles: 'like this'. We all set about our business, moving from one area to the next.

Old ladies with sleeves spanning from their wrists to their elbows, decorated with delicate flowers, worked with serious faces. They offered us their clothes, 'to protect your skin and keep clean whilst staying cool'. Lovely.

Coordinated groups worked more efficiently. We finished not too long after that.

Masanobu Tanaka (villager)
The experiences with the students made me realise how much people in Japan have been losing in exchange for our rapid economic growth. Overwork and less room in our minds has resulted in a society lacking in warm-hearted relationships between people. Material values and money have been controlling our minds without us really knowing it. Now we live in a society of crime and ill health. In contrast, the workshop students are not bound by time, they genuinely enjoy themselves. They are kind to old people and to children. They carefully observe the surrounding environment, and devote themselves to their work. I find in them something really important for life – something that we Japanese are striving to recover in our society.

26.8 Grass-cutting day with the elderly group

1-2.9 Maple Tree Festival

5.9 Public presentation at the Town Hall

25-26.8 Ueno Community Festival: costume contest

4.9 Preview of new spaces and farewell party

7.9 Cleaning day

27.8-2.9 Festival decoration

3-6.9 Building works on site

25-31.8 Construction work – four sites

tions with models

2001

Sven Stainer

Insects

The nights were hot and stuffy, and the natural impulse to open windows to let in some air was stifled by the abundance of insects. Wrapped in loose sheets so as not to expose too much skin, we carried our mattresses up to the roof, where the air was cooler and the constant slight breeze helped to get rid of the mosquitoes. The nights were calm, but far from quiet. Cicadas screeched with a reassuring regularity. The view from the roof revealed an incredibly deep, beautifully clear night sky.

Stargazing

I stumbled across a villager who had bought a telescope and spent numerous evenings watching the stars with interested locals and children. The school field was frequently used by boy scouts to camp during the summer months; this might have been a good place for stargazing. We thought of making a shelter for the telescope and an observation chair; a versatile platform, strong and compact to withstand the heavy snows in the winter, could unfold in the summer to protect the telescope from the wind and light. Specific events in the night sky were marked on a series of wooden walkways and then related to the landscape at a spot with the clearest views of the sky. The platform pointed south where most changes in the night sky occur, using the mountain silhouettes as a dramatic backdrop to frame the rising moon and sun throughout the year.

A circular concrete dish enabled the timber observation decks to rotate. The decks were tilted so we could lie on them, parallel to the sky. Metal bars were inserted into the smooth concrete to give a little resistance during the positioning and configuration of the swivel seat.

We drilled square holes with the help of four mechanical chisels and cut timber with Japanese thin-bladed saws, working at pull rather than push movements,

making a lot of the timber snap.

Supported on large, washed sandstones from the Shinano River, the timber screen supports were inserted into cuts scored in the stones. These then stood on concrete foundations submerged below the grass line, only exposing the rocks.

Japanese landscape

Winding roads through dense forests and rice paddies, passing heavily reinforced concrete embankments holding up the mountainsides; rough, geometric patterns of reinforcement and snow-retaining rigs swallowed by foliage gave us only a hint of what the winters here seemed to promise.

Shigeo Tanaka (villager)

Every summer when the students arrive, our quiet old place feels revitalised. The students help cut the grass of the old school field. We, in our old age, are constantly in awe of the powerful young arms slicing through the sea of grass, whereas they gasp in amazement to see us skilfully manoeuvre the lawn-mowers. Juicy watermelons are the break-time treat, and after the hot work, a cold beer goes down very well. Looking over the faraway mountain ranges, it is the moment when the differences in nationalities, languages and ages vanish. It really doesn't take long to feel close to each other; the realisation of which makes everyone smile.

Here in Koshirakura, curiosity towards the new has never been lost, while at the

17.8 Bon Festival dance and karaoke party

23.Gathering timber offcuts

24.8 Collecting thinned trees and rejected logs

22.8 Filming on location: Koshirakura Love Stories

23.8 Pinup presentations

25.8 Grass-cutting day with the elderly

26-28.8 Costume design and n

18-22.8 Project 1: Meeting place for two – five teams + five scenarios + five structures

23.8-7.9 Project 2: Roof for 200

23-29.8 Archive extension

23-31.8 Classroom conversion

same time our local traditions have been kept alive. During Momiji-hiki – our summer festival – no one escapes a soaking, whether from being thrown into carp ponds or splashed all over with buckets of water. Visiting households with celebrations such as a new birth or a new marriage in that year, we sing 'Tenjinbayashi' – our festival song with a unique heritage – and the family treats everyone to a feast in their garden. Although the whole thing appears riotous, there is an unspoken rule: no splashing water over the feast!

My hope is that the many students who stayed in our village share their experiences and memories with their friends and families on the other side of the planet. That way, our small community will have life through the connections of individual people.

2002

Pedro Jervel

Travelling to Koshirakura
It took over 20 hours to fly to Japan, half an hour to get from the airport to the train station and eight hours to reach Koshirakura by train and bus. In addition, there were some 20 hours of transit and delays. In total, I spent at least a day and a half travelling from my hometown to the village of Koshirakura.

Room for two
The first days were spent making small installations, temporary devices that would somehow be useful to the village. We made up a story in which Hiroshi-san, when he was young, dreamt that he had his own private forest and would climb the trees with his girlfriend to watch the sunset on the horizon. We designed and assembled a mechanism that operated by combining and balancing the impulse of movements between two people.

Live research
We continued documenting and exploring the place individually, socialising with local people, playing games and eating and drinking as we went along. I remember visiting wooden temples and looking at the amazing joinery, and being taken into a local family house. These served as references and stimuli for what we eventually built.

Matsuri
One of the most important events of the village, a religious ceremony, takes place in the month of August. Everybody helps, including us foreigners, by painting balloons and cutting down the biggest maple we can find – the tree is considered to be a symbol of prosperity. The festival is an opportunity for families who have had a special event in their lives to share their good fortune with the rest of the people. The tree is dragged around the village to the shrine, with many stops for eating, drinking and singing.

28.8 Ueno Festival costume performance contest (won 100 bottles of beer).

31.8-1.9 Home stay

6.9 Preview dinner under the roof

8.9 Main Maple Tree Festival, opening of Roof for 200

1.9 Reverse home stay dinner at the archive space

7.9 Maple tree cutting ceremony and fireworks

2-6.9 Setting up the Roof for 200

2.9 Gathering timber offcuts

9.9. Taking down the roof ceremony, bonfire

29.8 Open presentations

Costume competition

A costume big enough to dress the entire group. The whole structure moves, creating the choreography of a desperate mouth trying to catch a giant noodle with the help of a giant hand and giant chopsticks. These were constructed from wood, rice paper, chicken wire mesh and glue. We carried these over-scaled elements and ran around madly in front of the local audience.

Roof for 200

We were commissioned by the village to make a temporary structure to host the matsuri, designing it directly on site using timber off-cuts and pine branches. Negotiating with a local sawmill, and drawing on local knowledge of ways of binding things with rope, we joined the thin off-cuts by crossing them over and under each other as in a fabric structure. The resulting dome, festooned with giant paper lanterns, was spectacular, though on the day of the *matsuri* nobody dared to stand under it, for fear it would collapse.

2003

Ottilie Ventiroso

Building the Viewing Platform

How we constructed it – with a jig, maple tree, wood, details, measuring the site, laying lines, digging foundations, designing stuff, setting logs down, then measuring a graph of the line of the tree. The design utilised the natural curvature and strength of the beams, made of regular pieces of wood – Igawa-san. We looked at how the houses were constructed, their details, the shuttering systems, the high doorways above the snow line, the joint systems of the temple. The villagers liked the idea of a viewing platform under the tree, where they could sit and talk and look out across the valley. We designed a 3-m-long platform cantilevering out from the hillside and shaded by a large maple tree, whose roots were navigated around while laying the foundations. The terrain was extremely steep.

Tree cutting

Each year Kawanishi district sacrifices the largest maple tree, a natural system of sustainable forestry. Travelling into the woods to select a tree is an act of bravado and machismo, a quest to find the farmer with the biggest tree! Eventually, after several visits, a tree on a steep woodland bank was chosen. As per tradition, all the farmers and ourselves had a saw at the tree with a bread knife, spitting sake on the cut. The tree was carried to the village and placed in the centre of the square outside the temple, accompanied by a ritual dance relating to agriculture, fertility and landscape. Early the following morning a ceremony took place – *wachoi! wachi! wachi!* – and the tree was lowered down and taken to every household in the village for the blessing of a new venture – be it a birth, wedding or car. We were thrown into the carp pond before rejuvenating our tired limbs with hot sake and edamame. Folk songs were sung, some with pornographic lyrics, and young couples were forced to kiss each other in front of the whole village. Vik and I had to snog for the village elders twice – they'd never seen a french kiss before.

Adrian Priestman

Cicada and Snow*

To live for seven years under the ground
To emerge one night, screaming to find a mate
To hang upside down, and then in the space of two hours turn into a magnificent flying machine
To know how high up the side of a building to create your home, so as to be above the snow that settles up to six metres deep in the winter

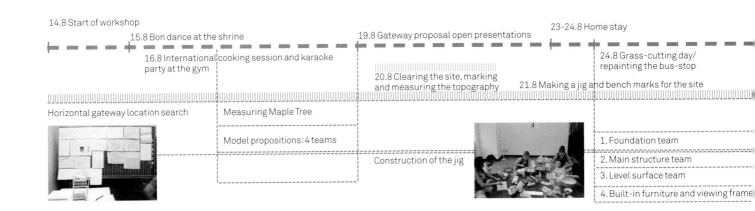

14.8 Start of workshop

15.8 Bon dance at the shrine

19.8 Gateway proposal open presentations

23-24.8 Home stay

16.8 International cooking session and karaoke
party at the gym

24.8 Grass-cutting day/
repainting the bus-stop

20.8 Clearing the site, marking
and measuring the topography

21.8 Making a jig and bench marks for the site

Horizontal gateway location search

Measuring Maple Tree

Model propositions: 4 teams

Construction of the jig

1. Foundation team
2. Main structure team
3. Level surface team
4. Built-in furniture and viewing frame

Grass-cutting

The smell of freshly cut grass combined with burning two-stroke oil and petrol. A team of people, working like locusts, descended on the voluptuously green pastures.

Food

Sour plums with sticky rice – a breakfast for champions. A sour plum is a mouthful that can turn your head inside out on first bite.

Horizontal gateway

A big maple, ceremoniously cut and carried, became the primary element for the Horizontal Gateway the following year – a shelter, a resting place, a platform. It frames a view. It holds stories of untold effort and frozen knowledge in every detail, learnt from structures that have seen hundreds of years.

26.8 Interim presentations

28.8. Costume performance rehearsals
29.8 Ueno town festival

6.9 Maple tree cutting
ceremony

9.9 Cleaning and
farewell party

|||||||||||||||||||||||||||||||||
Making river, bridge and fish costumes
for the annual contest in Ueno

1-5.9 Maple Tree Festival
preparations

7.9 Maple Tree Festival,
opening of Viewing Platform

25.8 Collecting foundation stones from
Shinano River. Planing offcut timber at
Igawa sawmill

Full-size mock-up on site

4.9 On-site assembly

10.9 Repainting
structures,
documentation

Site construction team

2.9 Casting foundations

Workshop construction team

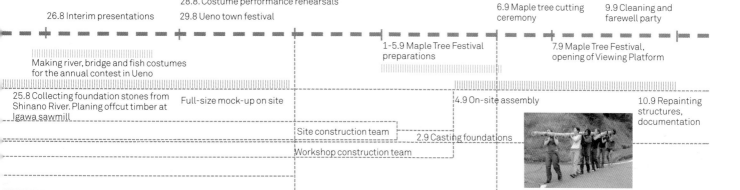

Seihan Watanabe (villager)

'Koshirakura is the place.' That was my response to Mr Sai Watanabe from the Niigata Regional Development Sector, when he rang me up and asked, 'Mr Shin Egashira, who currently teaches architecture in London, is to conduct a landscape workshop in a rural area in Niigata as part of the rural rejuvenation programme. Is there any good location for such an activity in Kawanishi?'

At the time the villages of Shirakura (Koshirakura and Oshirakura) were having difficulty finding alternative uses for their local school building, which had been closed for a couple of years. For instance a major corporation from the city had made an offer to convert the building into a resort facility, but the community preferred to keep the school for cultural or academic activities because it was still considered an important part of the life of the village. Shirakura has a reputation as a lively place. Although the population is small, there is a strong community spirit binding individuals, families and age groups. Unlike a typical rural village, where tradition and conservatism lead to a rejection of outsiders and change, this community is exceptionally outgoing. I thought this opportunity to host an architectural workshop with a group of international students would generate great excitement and help build up confidence within the community.

There were some concerns at the Town Hall. 'Would the village be used just as a research subject, a way of fulfilling their academic ambitions?' 'Would we end up introducing trouble into the community? They have never had the chance to meet foreigners before.... How would they react and communicate?'

These concerns soon disappeared when we met Mr Egashira and he immediately wanted to be introduced to the villagers. I was also relieved when I heard some residents of Koshirakura respond, 'Ho, foreign students. I am curious to see them.' Over a period of 10 years the workshop itself has become a new local tradition. Summers in Shirakura would not be complete without it. The relationship between the workshop and Koshirakura Village has become an inspiration for other villages.

Perhaps it suggests a unique model for the post-agricultural community in the twenty-first century.

2004

Matthew Murphy

Earthquake

The room felt like it was moving. The TV image, projected on the wall, became blurred and the columns started to bend. I felt sick and worried that my hangover was getting worse. I tried to steady myself on the floor but the room still moved – it was an earthquake. In Koshirakura, 160 miles away, buildings collapsed and roads folded like cardboard.

Arriving in Koshirakura

We walked up a corridor in the old school and past a kitchen, heading for the noise of chatting and children playing. Walking into the gym, we saw a hundred people sitting in circles, dishing out food and pouring beer, children jumping around. This was our welcome to the Koshirakura workshop; in a couple of weeks, we would all be connected.

Matsuri

Shintaro arrived by motorbike with a friend to find 50 drunk students and villagers huddled under the canopy of the house on the corner. Blocking the driveway was a large maple tree, tied with ropes and pieces of cloth. Branches and leaves littered the road that swung round and spilled precariously into the plot of each wooden

12.8 Initial meeting/review of previous year's projects

14.8 Bon dance at the shrine

13.8 Global BBQ party at the school gym

17-19.8 Filming local events

15-20.8 Project 1: three short films

19-20.8 Filming on location

A. On bus stop

B. In Azumaya

C. From Viewing Platform

house. Shin asked if we would introduce Shintaro to the pond. There were strings over the water with clothes-pegs holding doughnuts, and only minutes before we had been jumping up to grab them. Shintaro started his pleased-to-meet-yous, but before he could finish we had flung him into the black water. The fish were either hiding or had been removed, people were half-submerged or dripping at the edge, Shintaro was complaining of the cold and trying to be nice to the people he'd just met who had thrown him in. This was the fourth pond we had swum in so far.

Recycling
Afterwards Shin lined up all the cans from the entire stay. Like a theatrical giant, he walked on top of them, crushing them step by step.

The cinema screen
In the gym, intricate models had been made of the cinema structure, and the benefits of different joints were being hotly debated. Also, the strangest benches had been made out of old logs stained so that they looked just like fake logs. A dodgy moped ferried people back to the gym to check and re-check angles. In the dark, string was stretched, probably only semi-taut, and GCSE geometry was half-remembered as the foundations were marked out and the joint angles scribbled on scraps of paper.

People stood on top of the crossbeam and walked along it 20 ft above the old stone steps. There were only a few hours to go,

and the measurements were quite a bit out. Timber joints creaked as brute force and ignorance became the most common tools as the students strained to construct the screen. Some stayed behind in the dark and watched the school lights come on as a dinner of tempura was prepared by the nominated cooks.

The laughing face of the village shopkeeper was split into the several hundred pieces of string that formed the new Koshirakura Cinema. The cinema consisted of the steps of the shrine, a projector borrowed from the village hall and a string-and-timber screen that spanned the steps. The villagers were watching themselves in the adverts for the mushroom factory, the micro-parts workshop or the local petrol station.

School in the morning
The school was quiet in the morning, before breakfast, when people resemble more naturally their own nationality; sleep prevented affectation or social skill. Creeping around barefoot on the hard linoleum, finding 50 insects in the bathroom. The most annoying, and the smallest, were the mosquitoes, but there were also giant moths frozen against the walls, stick insects on the window ledges, beetles in the corridors.

Film
1. Nighttime edits
By 2.00 am most people were asleep or gossiping on the roof, trying not to get eaten

by the mosquitoes. Two were hunched over laptops inside, facing the pool that is slowly filling with water. Haphazardly dressed, they edited footage for several hours. The films were of possessed houses that collapse and expand as if controlled by ghosts, of time-bending bus stops and magic water wells, muddied explorers climbing through paddies.

2. Shooting footage
From the roof you could see out across the village to the bridge under construction. Several students were already walking along the road on the other side of the valley, going off to make a film. They placed screens across the valley to reflect views over the village and beyond the next hill, and as they climbed through wet plants and sticky mud they found an abandoned baby-blue Suzuki, overgrown and rusted. On their way home they met a chubby kid on his bike who circled them without saying a word.

Costume competition: the fruit salad
We wound the old van up over the hills towards the town, with everybody knocking into each other in the back. Tied to the roof were huge tomatoes, grapes and other fruits, and a 12-ft-long knife made of tin foil. For the Koshirakura Workshop, the troupe performed the 'Fruit Salad' – an intricate dance which had taken days to prepare and which culminated in the chopping in half of the two tomato performers.

20-21.8 Home stay   22.8 Grass-cutting day with the elderly group   25.8 Ueno Festival

23-25.8 Design and making of costumes for Ueno Festival

22-27.8 Project 2: Staging scenarios/construction of props. Three teams

A. Storyboard 'Koshirakura Story'

B. Constructing fictional props

C. Designing a local cinema screen

Grass-cutting

Everybody arrived at the school early in the morning. Those of us who stayed with Tanaka-san arrived in a better mood than the other students, but then we'd had beer for breakfast. All the men wielded deadly strimmers. By afternoon, the grass had all been cut and overturned structures righted; now we could move on to the real purpose of the day – the party. From the school roof there was a perfect view of the blue sheet party 30 ft below. There was one big circle on the right, with some people spilling onto a smaller sheet and half-empty beer crates in the middle. In a smaller circle of girls there was an even smaller circle of glasses and plates.

Rubens Azevedo

Koshirakura

Inside a bus, just the driver with his driver's cap and me with my bag. I looked at the landscape and the driver looked at me through the rearview mirror. I looked at him and he smiled – he knew exactly where I was going. I looked at the landscape; I had seen it before, but only in films. The difference now was the smell of rice. I was inside the school, alone. As I explored the building, I was followed all the while by a bee. The bee and I took photographs.

Suddenly a tune boomed out from a loudspeaker, and even the bee disappeared at that moment. It was morning; I was hungry and I went to look for the source of the sound – it was the terrace on top of the

school. From the terrace I could see the valley and the village for the first time. Somehow the discovery of the speaker was my first project in Koshirakura.

International food fair

I was asked to produce food from my own country as an offering to the villagers. So my second project in Koshirakura was to make *brigadeiro*, a Brazilian children's party sweet made of cocoa, butter, condensed milk and chocolate coating. It was a disaster (I'd never tried to make it before), but the village people seemed to like it. I drank, I talked, I drank, I sang a duet of 'Let It Be' and I sang in Japanese. Fortunately the speaker was never on in the evenings.

Costume competition

I dressed as a lamp bulb and girls dressed as insects flew around me – and were smashed with a certain pleasure by a gigantic flip-flop with a cigarette dangling between his lips, à la Belmondo.

Cinema screen

Woken up by the speaker instead of the rooster, we set to designing and producing a prop. Ours was a screen, a portable white canvas, a white reflector, an orientation device, a communication network. We made a film about the prop but the prop proved more cinematic than the film. The props were not to be shown, they were there to be used. I should have known that, it's so Herzog.

For relaxation we played volleyball on the volleyball court. There were cigarettes, there was rain and there was beer.

I was doing options for joints for the screen; it was to be a dry joint, a system of pieces that would interlock without the need for either screws or nails: technically known as *CRIK*. I worked on the base of the structure, the columns and the beams. The screen was to be positioned opposite the shrine and parts of it would cantilever over a slope. There were four foundations – two for the two columns and two for the anchoring elements, the two beams, which worked both ways: in tension and in compression. One year later someone forgot about that detail and the whole structure collapsed.

The foundations of the structure were to be positioned in an irregular trapezoidal configuration. The two sides were of different sizes and would meet the columns at an angle. The screen was to be parallel to the steps leading to the shrine: from below it would appear as a gate, from above as a screen. We made a 1:1 sketch model of the structure and positioned it in the site. Through triangulation we measured the angles at which the beams would meet the columns. I would have to carve a rectangular slot through a 20 x 20 cm log; the slot had to be at an angle.

We drew a section on rice paper in red ink and pencil. We placed the structure inside the volleyball court, but the angles could only be checked on site.

More volleyball, more cigarettes, more rain, more speakers, more dinners, more beer, more sake, more wake up, more cleaning, more cooking, more cigarettes, more beer, more sake. The angles were, with the help of a hammer, correct. The structure went up and the screen unfurled like the sail of a boat. The strings of the screen moved beautifully in the wind. A stronger wind would have made everything collapse. Morning, and we sat in front of the shrine and drank sake and beer out of waterproof containers – yellow, red, white, everybody had one. We chopped down a 90-year-old maple tree. It was close to a dangerous bee's nest, but we chopped it down anyway and dragged it around. Then we watched a film on our screen.

5.9 Maple Tree Festival

8.9 Farewell party and final screening

7.9 Cleaning day

9-11.9 Repairing the Bus Shelter and Local Archive

9.9. Storing the cinema structures

Last day

Everybody left and we carried out some maintenance on the old structures. We painted the bus stop. There were some bees inside, which were violently gassed and hammered down with Japanese precision. We made a bench on the viewing platform. I smoked a cigarette and played baseball inside the volleyball court. Domo Domo Domo.

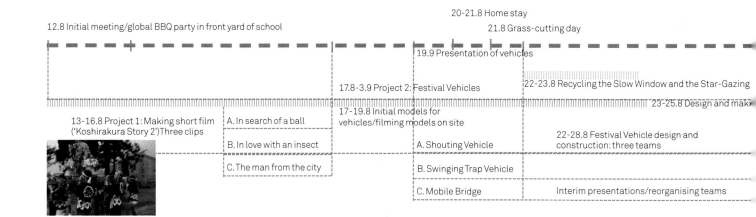

12.8 Initial meeting/global BBQ party in front yard of school

20-21.8 Home stay

21.8 Grass-cutting day

19.9 Presentation of vehicles

17.8-3.9 Project 2: Festival Vehicles

22-23.8 Recycling the Slow Window and the Star-Gazing

13-16.8 Project 1: Making short film ('Koshirakura Story 2') Three clips

A. In search of a ball

B. In love with an insect

C. The man from the city

17-19.8 Initial models for vehicles/filming models on site

23-25.8 Design and maki

A. Shouting Vehicle

22-28.8 Festival Vehicle design and construction: three teams

B. Swinging Trap Vehicle

C. Mobile Bridge

Interim presentations/reorganising teams

2005

Krishan Pattni

a. Wasabi on a piece of cucumber
Arriving disoriented in the humid night, a week late, we found ourselves being led up the hill to a house, where, upon removing our shoes, we found a great dinner under way. Here two significant discoveries were made: 1. There are a large variety of things in traditional Japanese cuisine for a vegetarian. 2. Green paste on an innocent looking piece of cucumber makes your eyes water. The evening progressed with stories from the previous nine years of workshops. Haruo-san remembered every name from the past. Sitting cross-legged on the tatami around the low table we could catch glimpses through the sliding screens into the busy kitchen and beyond, to the silhouetted hills in the distance. Instantly we felt at home.

b. The gym
A space divided in two: one half still operated as a basketball court, the other was a blue-tarpaulin-covered timber workshop. The workshop had of a series of hand tools (mainly Japanese saws, chisels and mallets) as well as a circular saw, two jig saws, three Makitas, one pillar drill and one mortise drill. Gradually the blue tarpaulin disappeared under a thick layer of sawdust.

At the end of the room, near by the stage, three people were stitching together the plywood shell of a 2-m-long horn. To their left four others stood atop their seat bridge, testing its load-bearing capacity as it spanned between two tables. In the front of the room a little production line was in action. Five people were beaverishly chiselling 250 square holes, 25 x 25 mm, for the louvered panels of a fold-out toy box. Two lay asleep on the dusty polished wooden floor in the midst of tools and a selection of Japanese timber joints from a recycled structure. Most people worked barefoot. The space was softened by the constant presence of two little girls and Shun from the village, swinging on the exercise ropes and running around trapping grasshoppers with bits of timber.

c. Lanterns in the rain!
It was the night before the festival and a group of us were at the village shrine two-thirds of the way down the hill. We were helping to hang the last of the hand-painted paper lanterns over the clearing in front of the temple. The cinema screen had been assembled earlier in the day and images of the village flickered above us. The men from the village helped with the last preparations, as the women went home to get dressed for the festivities and the evening dance. A large lantern wall stood immediately in front of the shrine.

Moments before the event began, a crack of thunder brought a downpour of warm rain. Everyone rushed for shelter under the large eaves of the temple, and here a new event took place – huddled together and stranded in a 1.2-m-wide space around the perimeter of the temple, 30 of us watched the rain through a screen of lanterns. It soaked the paper first, then softened the light; slowly the beautifully delineated trees, mountains and dragonflies washed away onto the bare earth in front of the shrine and down the long steep stone steps into the basin of the village. All that remained was the yellow glow of the 40W bulbs with the white glow of the screen in the background, filtering through the thick grey curtain of rain. Gusts of strong wind animated the structures. There was a dance after all!

d. Festival vehicles
The day of the tree festival arrived. After eating riceballs (some containing a wasabi surprise) and getting thoroughly drenched in the school swimming pool, the villagers set off down the long main road to the village for more 'drenchings', food, sake and laughter. From the school, the whole event and the three weeks of life in Koshirakura united in a view of the procession rolling down the hill. The plywood trumpet led, blaring a rhythmic *wa-choi* and spraying anyone in its territory with its water cannon. The Toy-Box and Bridge followed, forming the festival train. Behind it the locomotive power of the village members mixed with students was bound to a 40-mm-diameter rope dragging the 7-m-long, 60-year-old maple tree down the hill. This combination

23-25.8 Design and making of costumes (18 sheep) for Ueno Festival Sheep dance practice

28.8 Play day with 30 local children from Tachibana Primary School
1. Origami and drawing class 2. Cooking class
3. Play with vehicles

5-6.9 Cleaning days

3.9 Maple tree cutting ritual at the mountain Festival eve volleyball match: village v workshop

26-30.8 Maple Tree Festival preparations

4/9 Maple Tree Festival with three new vehicles

ce practice

29.8-2.9 Final construction phase of vehicles

6.9 Farewell party at the community house. Film screening 'Koshirakura Story 2'

1-4.9 Joined by architects from Maeda Corporation, Tokyo

of shared energy and laughter around the structures we had constructed formed a beautiful architecture, a new culture for that moment.

Haruo Eguchi (villager)

During the workshop, it became my daily routine to come and see you all, joining the late suppers and then talking, sometimes to midnight. Before we knew it, one month of brief but rich encounters mounted up to 10. How quickly the years have gone by! I wonder how all the students are – each of you is alive and shining in my memory.

On 23 October 2004 the first big tremor of the earth forced us all out into the open, then the second and the third ones struck. Our houses were creaking, the roof tiles falling like thunder; I was praying that our house would survive. The aftershocks gradually proceeded towards us – with a horrifying boom accompanied by rustling leaves. We were struck motionless with fear. It was a cold night and I went in to get something to wear – everything was scattered, but somehow I managed to salvage some blankets and overcoats. The whole village gathered in the community centre where the students stay during the summer. It was a sleepless night with recurring tremors. I never felt more thankful than when I saw the sun rise the next day. Looking back, it was a terrible year. However, people in Koshirakura gradually regained their courage, and were able to greet the students again in the summer.

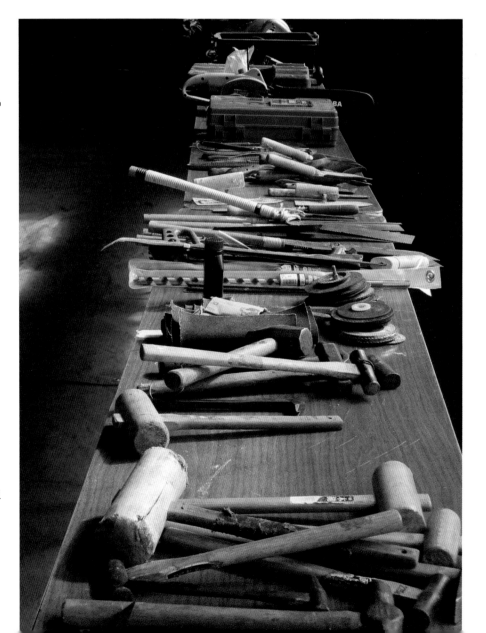

20.8 Grass-cutting day with elderly group followed by Azumaya party

18.8. First day, cleaning the school

20.8 Evening BBQ party at the school car park

29.8 Blues concert at the gym

21.8 Setting up the Cinema Screen at the shrine

21.8 Setting up the workshop at gym

19.8 Project 1: Haiku reading, 6 teams, 12 haiku, 12 locations, 12 pictures

24.8 First visit to Senjyu Onsen

Repair works for the Cinema Screen

Project 2: Roof over the shrine

20.8 Very short Haiku films by four teams

21.8 Sketch proposal presentations by four groups: full-scale and non-scale details

22.8 Harvesting excess bamboo from local backyards

23.8 Late night project meeting in the gym

20.8 Short film preview

26.8 Sumo performance
at Ueno Festival

4.9 Play-day with a class of 18 students
from Tachibana Primary School
1. Origami and drawing class 2. Cooking
class 3. Play with vehicles

25-26.8 Making a couple of sumo
wrestlers out of bamboo strips

28-30.8 Momiji festival decoration works at
the communal house

5.9 A day of cleaning

26.8 Party with Ueno
Seinendan

29.8 Wood planing at Igawa sawmill

30-31.8 Setting up bamboo, tree joint and
pulley details on three trees in the shrine

Three teams:

28.8 Measuring the site and tree trunks

4.9 Farewell Party at the
community house

A: Tree and bamboo hinge details

30.8 Full scale roof mock up on site

B: Roof textile

30.8-1.9 Stitching up blue-and-white tarpaulin sheets (total length 195 m) n

6.9 A day of filming by Rubens

C: Swing seat for the shrine cinema

30.8 Casting foundations for pivoting bench

1.9 Building the roof in vertical position, structure
and tarpaulin fabric patterns

Chapter 4   Events and Networks

Festivals and Enclosed Systems

Eupkecha: an insect in a story by Kobo Abe; a super-sustainable beetle. It consumes, digests, discharges and cultivates simultaneously within a small circle the diameter of its body length. It rotates at regular intervals and speeds. Eupkecha is the clock of the village. It regulates rhythms and shows the time to eat, work and sleep. There is an annual festival in Koshirakura during the mating season of the eupkecha. As the beetles fly away to find partners for a couple of weeks, time disappears from the village.

There are many ways of telling the time in Koshirakura, not just the clock with loud-speakers in the former school: the depth of the snow, the colours of the trees, the length of the rice stalks. Each clock indicates timings of collective activities and events during the year. They all seem to have a practical use. Ordinary things such as grass-cutting, rope-making and harvesting are directly related to the necessary activities of the farming community as a ritualised form of land maintenance.

In the winter of 2001, I went with a group of AA students to a traditional winter festival, called Baito, in Oshirakura, the village next to Koshirakura. Like the Maple Tree Festival, Baito is a collective form of consuming excess; people use the ritual in order to rewind or adjust their clocks against other clocks.

At six in the morning on 15 January a 20-m-diameter circle was dug out of the snow in the middle of the community. The edge of the circle was compressed to form a foundation for tree branches that were stood vertically upon it, at close intervals all the way around the circle. Layer upon layer of branches was built up, tied together with straw ropes.

By midday a 20-m-high cone-shaped structure had emerged. Then we began covering the volume of the cone with bundles of straw until we had made an enclosure with a single entrance just large enough for one person to pass though.

By 6 pm there was a small bonfire in the centre of the interior space, with huge vats of dark soup cooking – a mixture of unknown ingredients, presumably vegetables and pig intestines, etc. Sitting around the bonfire were circles of approximately 150 people, including our group. We ate and drank a lot of sake and sang the Oshirakura version of 'Tenjinbayashi'.

By 8 pm the interior of this big powwow became some sort of sweathouse, producing lively noises dampened by the heavy snow. At 8.30 pm the villagers began to add more and more piles of straw to the fire. As the fire got bigger more people had to get out. By the time the last group left, the flames were as tall as the structure.

Now the circle of people had regrouped outside the structure, which was about to become a very big fire in the middle of the village. It was rather overwhelming, as the whole landscape of snow reflected the orangeness of the fire. The festival finished when the structure collapsed into a black spot.

Everyone began to tidy up the mess and clear up all the things left from this ritual, as if it was an everyday routine. All the locals went home, perhaps to catch their favourite TV programme. We were left standing in front of a black spot in the middle of snow, still trying to make sense of what we had experienced that day.

Shirakura Festivals

Bon, Grass-Cutting Day, Momijihiki, Jimankai, Snow-Sculpture Competition, Baito, Cherry Festival

In a place like Koshirakura environmental forces refine the forms of all the built structures as well as the shape of the land. These unchangeable climatic forces, as well as the limited economy of such a rural community, made us think of the meaning of design. Whatever is built as part of this environment automatically demands continuous maintenance and care. Accumulated snow must be removed during the winter period.

As the population gets older, the capacity for maintenance is naturally reduced. For instance the croquet team no longer exercises on the field we provided with the Slow Window in 1998, so the ground only reveals its designed contours once a year, when we do the grass-cutting event together with the older villagers.

The Slow Window did not survive the earth-quake and heavy snows of 2004. In the summer of 2005 we had to make a decision to take it down rather than reconstruct it. The Star-Gazing Platform only remains in the form of its footprint for the same reason.

I noticed the notion of distance begin to emerge even within the local scale. The ground these structures were standing on is the highest terrain behind the school building, which requires more effort to reach even though it is only a matter of 150 m horizontally, and 10 m vertically, from the centre of the village, where the shrine is located. I felt that we had to revise the previous map that indicated the size and outline of Koshirakura. On the playground we made a pile of scrap timber from the structures, and after sorting out the pieces we could reuse, set it on fire. The flames went up much higher than expected when the chief of the year threw petrol over them (an illegal act, even in such a remote environment).

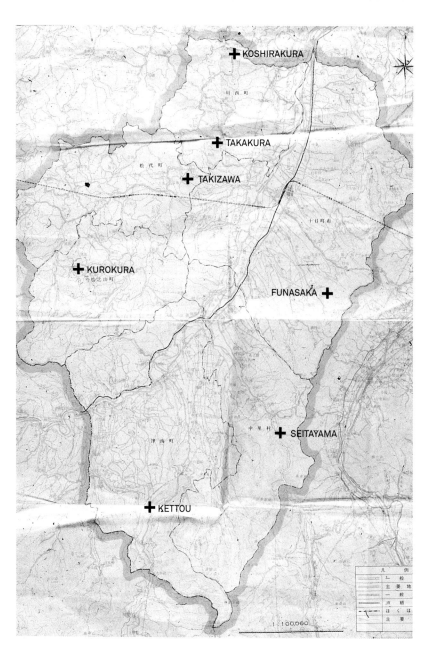

The Slow Box travelled aound six villages and one town in the Tsumari district.

Project for the Tsumari
Art Triennale 2000
Fram Kitagawa
(Executive Director)
Shin Egashira
(Project Director)
Naohisa Yabuta
(Coordination)

Construction Team
(April 2000)
Aoi Kume
Shuji Mizukami
Yasushi Takahashi
Atsuko Oikawa
Momoko Kawata
Eiji Yoshida
Ryu Tsuchiya
Asao Tokoro

Journey / Afterimage
Workshop Collaborators
(July 2000);
Ema Bonafacic
Maria Chung
Phoebe Dakin
Suk-Kyu Hong
Koichiro Ioka
Anna Kubelic
Aoi Kume
Julia Mauser
Inigo Minns
Shuji Murakami
Bart Schoonderbeck
Demos Simatos
Yasushi Takahashi
Takakura Village of
Kawanishi Town
Takizawa Village
of Matsudai Town
Kurokura Village of
Matsunoyama Town
Kettou Village of
Tsunan Town
Seitayama Village
of Nakazato Village
Funasaka Village
of Toukamachi city
Koshirakura Village
of Kawanishi Town

Material sponsored by
Maeda Corporation

Equipment supplied by
Igawa Corporation

Slow Box, After Image

In 2000 the first international art triennale in Tsumari District of Niigata (made up of seven towns and cities including Kawanishi Town) was planned. Its director, Fram Kitagawa of Art Front Gallery, invited me to contribute a project for this event, with a request for a proposal that would inform links between seven towns and cities in the Tsumari District. We would make artworks in the form of a documentary requiring local participation. The idea quickly evolved into a project with three stages.

One: making an object that would register the climate and aspects of the places.

Two: using the object as a tool (vehicle) to communicate with various participants, including local residents in a form of workshop.

Three: making an installation to document the transformation of objects as well as the events of communication.

The proposal, in short, required the fabrication of a large camera vehicle that could capture aspects of the landscape and the people who live with it. It was meant be over-sized so that a person could fit inside. Metaphorically, it was to work like an eupkecha – as a wooden beetle made with traditional farmhouse details, which would travel through the villages of Tsumari every three years. The size of the camera was articulated by the proportional relationship between objects, the size of the picture plane, the diameter of the aperture and the distance between them. As a result it required an exposure time of between 15 and 30 minutes in daylight conditions. The direct print (imprint) size is 1.5 x 1.5 m square on a 5 mm toughened glass pane coated with photo emulsion.

This wooden beetle, which we call a Slow Box, produces a series of after images by absorbing light and consuming it through a photosynthetic process. With the help of Shuji Mizukami and Asao Tokoro, the Slow Box was constructed in the wood store lent by Igawa Corporation in Kawanishi, using materials donated by the Maeda Corporation.

We planned the itinerary by asking each town to recommend their most beautiful village/community in a difficult-to-reach location. Seven villages showed their interest in collaborating, namely Takakura, Takizawa, Kurokura, Kettou, Seitayama, Funasaka and Koshirakura. The workshop was organised in the form of a tour with three to four days in each village. We used Koshirakura as our base, returning there from time to time to develop large negatives on glass. The journey was planned to start in early July and finish at the beginning of August, to coincide with the regular Koshirakura workshop.

A Documentary of Documenting

Taking photographs became a ritualistic form of communication that required no complex explanations. We were just like ordinary tourists asking permission to take photographs in different countries. But here, the size of the camera was important: it had to be big enough to be taken seriously.

Opposite above: Slow Box elevation drawing.

Opposite below: Slow Box skeleton model showing how the structure can flip from a horizontal position (when it is in transit or being used as a darkroom) to a vertical fixed position, which allows one to sit inside and see the inverted image.

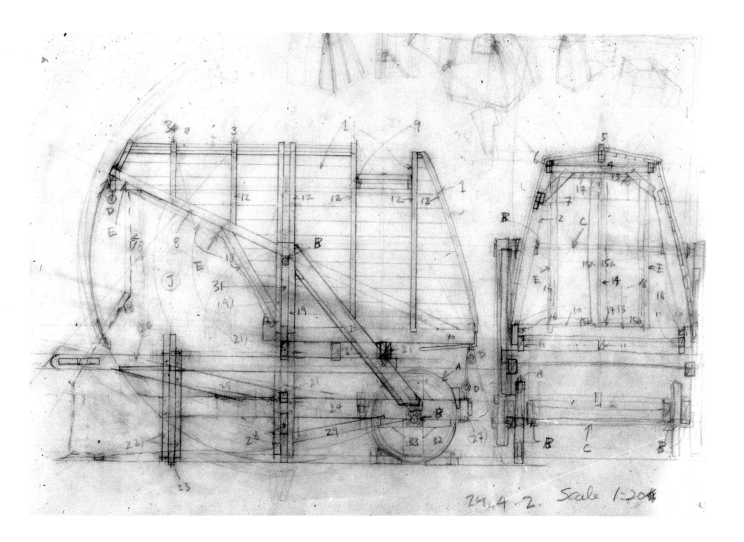

Funaska Village, 29 July 2000

Inigo Minns / Inside the Slow Box

We have built a huge darkroom on the stage of the Koshirakura school hall, the red velvet curtains sealed shut with tape to keep the light out. It's hot and pitch black and the thick air is filled with the fumes of developing fluids. As it turns out, we will all spend a lot of time sweating in the dark over the next few weeks.

I switch on the red light, and in the dim glow three of us begin to unwrap the first of the huge sheets of light-sensitive glass. In a short period we go from being dry to sodden, our clothes sticking to us with a mixture of sweat and developing fluids as we go through the process of transferring onto the glass the images taken earlier in the day. Quite suddenly, and to our great relief, they appear. In front of our eyes we can see dark and light smudges emerge on the glass and quickly turn into the lines and forms of the people, trees and buildings from that morning.

A large team of volunteers in collaboration with a number of villages in the area have spent a lot of time and energy trying to document the people of this part of Niigata in these large-scale group portraits; and up until this moment it was not clear whether it would work. We came here to document the area at a time of change. As more and more young people move to the nearby towns, the traditions and way of life are being maintained by fewer and fewer elderly locals.

The camera itself was the product of a mixture of research and informed guesswork. At first sight I could hardly understand what I was looking at, let alone see which bit of it could possibly take a photograph. The thing in front of me somehow resembled a huge dung beetle rearing up on its hind legs – a beetle built from large blackened timbers by a nineteenth-century shipwright … and set on wheels. The intention was to haul the beetle-camera from village to village, where it would be positioned and made steady and level. This required the main body to be tilted upright, a job usually for four or five people, in a motion similar to someone straightening up after having just touched their toes. After this, its huge timber arms were secured with ropes to stop it falling back down. At this point the subject matter, normally a collection of elderly rice farmers and their families, would position themselves in front of the camera on tiered seating against a backdrop of hills, fields and timber and mud houses or stores. When everything was in place someone had to climb inside the camera, seal it shut and expose the sheet of light-sensitive glass to the image that was being projected onto it through a pin prick in the face of the camera.

Over time we all began to build up a close relationship with the thing as we hauled it daily from one village to the next, in a procession akin to a medieval pilgrimage caravan bearing a precious effigy. How strange it must have seemed to the elderly villagers we visited as an increasingly dishevelled troupe of people from all over the world turned up in a slow-moving convoy of car, van and tiny buzzing moped, with the tractor bearing the camera at the centre, raised up high and sheathed in canvases lashed with ropes for protection.

Climbing down into the belly of the camera for the first time as it creaked and shook around me, I felt like an early pioneer about to descend into the depths of the ocean in some kind of prototype submarine. Last waves and smiles to those outside before closing up the hatch and sinking into my own world of muffled sounds and stifling darkness. Once inside, some necessary instructions had to be shouted through the timber walls. Is everyone in place and still? Countdown from 5 … carefully cut the protective paper off the light-sensitive glass to expose the pinhole image onto it … and then silence. It's a long hour.

Perched uncomfortably on one of the timber beams in as little clothing as possible, accompanied only by a bottle of water, a knife and the upside-down image projected through the pinhole onto the glass above my head, it's easy for the mind to wander. The night before comes swimming into view: the same people now static above my head had last night been singing and laughing into the early morning. Each village we visited had prepared a celebration that usually began with formal speeches and ended with drunken karaoke. It was the swiftly following hangover that was sweated out inside the baking oven of the camera the next day.

As the words for 'Love Me Tender' drifted through my mind I could feel the residual alcohol seep out of my pores. Watching those outside, sitting still in the sunshine I wondered what they were thinking. There was something wonderful about this time, all this stillness and thought being focused into this single act. As the light is not strong enough to catch the moment instantly (unlike a camera with a lens that intensifies the light) the subjects must remain completely still for long periods for the pinhole camera to capture the portrait. Not so much capturing an instant as capturing an hour. An infinite number of instances channelled through that pin prick to form an image of the passage of time. Somehow it becomes more than the hour of stillness and heat. It is two groups of strangers meeting and sharing something, the camera acting as catalyst translating so many disparate experiences into a single common image.

The pictures were eventually displayed in an old hall with tall windows high up on a remote hillside. Twenty or so large sheets of glass with images showing the people of this quiet corner of Japan, the sepia colour and hazy focus conjuring up anthropological images that could have been taken a hundred years before. And yet some of the images are almost completely obscured; no more than the brown whorls and clouds of the developing process with the odd almost discernible feature. It is as if some aspects of this rural world have slipped through our fingers, just as the fading traditions in the area that we were trying to record may already be lost to future generations.

Returning to Koshirakura at the end of the project a friend and myself were lucky enough to spend some time with Eguchi-san and his family. Three generations living under one roof manage to farm the land, breed prize-winning carp and produce micron-accurate parts for Harley Davidson motorbikes in a modern-day cottage industry run from the house. After a tour of the area in a large 4x4, following our progress on a dashboard-mounted Sat Nav, I was dressed in the thick silk gown traditionally worn by men in the region and sat down to one of the largest and most colourful meals I have ever eaten. Dish after dish of every shape and hue appeared on the table until it was completely covered. A multicoloured spread of almost unrecognisable but delicious edibles: Raw beef, sea urchins, sticky moulding beans, tempura vegetables … and the common language of whisky and sake. As we sat around with the huge TV blaring out some Saturday night game show we all began to relax – the visitors in traditional dress and our hosts in jeans and T-shirts. Hiroshi, the family member closest to my own age, eventually took us up to his room where he played us his guitar and we sang into the night. He liked the classic rock ballads, while we were trying to learn the words for the local village song handed down through the generations. And that is the reality of what we were documenting. I'm not sure whether Hiroshi would be able to make one of the raincoats, thatched from rice grass, that one of the older women of Koshirakura showed me … but I know that he'd give it a good go.

Seitayama Village, 26 July 2000

Takakura Village, 13 July 2000

Takizawa Village, 15 July 2000

Koshirakura Village, 10 July 2000

Takizawa Village, 16 July 2000

Arriving at Takakura Village, 12 July 2000

Funasaka Village, 28 July 2000

Funasaka Village, 29 July 2000

Koshirakura Village, 31 July 2000

Kettou Village, 21 July 2000

Koshirakura Village, 21 July 2000: loading a 1.5 x 1.5 m glass pane coated with
photo emulsion and wrapped in a sleeve of black paper to take a single shot.

Adiam Sertzu / Tsumari Journey

bamboo toy propeller – Koshirakura
kenichisan sitting in old school dining room
grinning
sharp carving knife
bold slices
with skilled spontaneous hands
flying bamboo flakes shavings

pinhole camera – Takakura
cardboard boxes small cans
cigarette boxes and torn wrapping
spiders cobwebs dust and glossy paper
red headlights duck-tape-sealed darkroom
heavy fumes

pumpkin-kabocha – Takizawa
village ladies preparing lunch
rushing talking laughing
tasting scolding
arranging rice balls positioning
edamame pickled plums and ginger

crane – Kurokura
old lady sitting over low table
folding cranes from bright magazine cuttings
shoeboxes full

dinner party at night in town hall – Tachibana
children running around colliding with
laughing screaming on tatami
overturned cups spilt sake

made nothing-just looked – Seitayama
four old men in hard hats sweeping
little road curving up a hill
small intricate houses rich dark stained wood
dark square ponds with grills
swimming
with bright ginger-orange carp

color purple – Funasaka
sarah cutting leather
lady with husband
beautiful house old loom inside
soft untwisted yarn light silk thin silk
weaving and dyeing
out in back garden small shrubs and herbs
big ruffled tinted leaves deep burgundy
shiso
pull out shake and wash off soil
tear leaves off stem
soak in water
boil
until red shiso leaves turn greenish
until water is dark bluey-purple.
drain leaves keep water
add little rice vinegar
intense magenta pink flush
put in piece of leather
leave
fix add salt
hang dry
wait for colour
wait for shade
wait for tone

Old lady with *yugao* melon, Takakura Village, July 2003

2003 Slow Box
and After Image
Hiroshi Eguchi
Akiharu Ogino
Anna Shevel
Sarah Entwistle
Adiam Sertzu
Farah Azizan
Ottilie Ventiroso
Lena Tutunjian
Chan Zhi Xiong
Ko Matoba
Igawa Kazuhiro
Adrian Priestman

Shin Egashira

In 2003, three years after the first camera journey, the second tour was conducted. Our intention was to trace the same route, following the same schedule and finding the same locations in the villages we had photographed three years before.

There were two new cameras, a suitcase camera for small group portraits, equipped with a single-2 cm-diameter magnifying glass with a manual focus mechanism and four different apertures to choose from. An old suitcase from Oxfam was converted by means of a folding mechanism so that one could wear it and become a part of the camera as the picture was taken. The other camera was a pinhole panoramic camera ideal for landscapes or for individual portraits.

The journey didn't turn out quite as we had expected. We found more opportunities to shoot small groups (for example families, friends, couples, workgroups), but it was harder to get whole communities together (more people seemed to be working outside the villages). We used the suitcase camera more often than expected. The exception was Tachibana village, which wanted to involve local schoolchildren in the project.

Suitcase camera: translation from a camera suit into a trolley.
Its journey also included a flight from London to Narita airport.

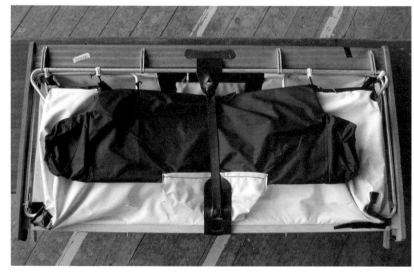

Top: Landscape-format camera, suitcase camera and Slow Box
together in Takakura school gym.

Bottom left: Landscape-format camera folded up.
Bottom right: Suitcase camera in a house at Funasaka Village.

Ottilie Ventiroso

Arriving in Koshirakura

The music of xylophones resonates across the tree-lined valley where the village of Koshirakura lies. Lush terraced plateaus of rice paddies cover the slopes; the harvest is still unripe, a zinging pale green in the twilight. The mist settles as the last light fades. There is no one to be seen. The bus stop is oddly familiar, reminiscent of Ching's Yard at the AA.

Pinhole Camera

We are at the beginning of Slow Box/After Image – a journey around six villages in the Tsumari mountain district in Niigata where we will capture the faces of the farming folk, young and old, using elaborate pinhole cameras. We drive to Takakura, 50 miles from Koshirakura.

We establish a makeshift darkroom in a little-used school gym using tatami, curtains and rolled up cardboard to block out the sunshine. Our lab is lightless and airless, characterised by the acrid smell of photographic solution and unventilated, sweltering heat. We make ambitious pinhole cameras with matches and cardboard boxes, learning about focal length and pinhole diameter ratio, apertures, exposure and development. We play in the village with our new cameras – botanical *daikon* and *shizo* macro-shot, agricultural machinery landscape, old hunchback lady portrait. Climbing into the photo sauna through a shutter on a staircase, we wear bikinis and sarongs to develop, stop and fix our pinhole experiments, submerging the paper in baking trays with chopsticks. Proud grey photos are hung on washing lines to dry. Contrast improves over the next 100 exposures.

Takizawa Village Portrait

1　Meeting the village

Takizawa is the first village we travel to. The chief greets and welcomes us into the community house, where a group of villagers have gathered and are preparing a feast. I sit with a calligrapher, a *shodo* painter. We spontaneously take out brushes and ink, and he explains the art of painting, drawing *kanji* for us. Singing, Asahi, and 'the best sake in the world!' follow late into the night.

2　The photograph

At 10 am the next day, the villagers converge, while a suitcase unfolds to construct and reveal a sit-in pinhole camera. In the cloaked pitch blackness I blindly push my arms through sleeves and grasp a thread which opens the shutter. I see the whole village upside down, smiling boldly in the morning light. Tiny children sit on tricycles near their parents, but the majority are of a different generation. All have the same wonder in their eyes as they watch this multinational group operate these obscure puppet-like devices. The villagers draw closer into the view of the lens. The shutter is closed as I fumble to place a photographic sheet on the screen above me, hopefully the right way around.

A muffled voice calls a light reading and the exposure time. People count down outside and I pull the shutter open, estimating 1.46 seconds. We take another just to be safe – it would be a shame to lose this. Compared to a risk-free digital machine, these archaic imprecise cameras are a refreshing gamble. *Ichigo Ichie.* Treasure every meeting, for it will never recur.

Ice-Cream Bus

We travel back to Takakura after tea at the shodo painter's house. Strange dreamlike music wafts through the window, and Shin runs outside, chasing its source. It's the Japanese equivalent of Mr Whippy – the Tofu Van.

Takakura Village

In the evening we head down to the community centre of Takakura for another raucous party, of sushi and sashimi, karaoke, massage chairs and the overwhelming pleas of '*dozo! dozo!*'

from generous villagers wanting to refill glasses, and the inevitable downing of huge amounts of 'the best sake in the world!' Next morning, the dawn chorus plays out on the megaphones, the village arrives and the documentation process is repeated. Later I wander into the woods to find, hidden in foliage, tiny bear cubs living in the roof of a collapsed building. I notice how many houses have been left empty, abandoned for urban migration.

Photographing the Children

At 1 am Shin asks, 'Ottilie, can you make 300 children sit still for a 10-minute exposure tomorrow morning?' We could get them to balance plates on their heads or construct a jig to hold them still...

In the end we come up with a strategy of making them play musical statues as a rehearsal for the photograph. A little band was quickly formed and various instruments gathered from around the school – Lena grabbed some frying pans, Xiong made an impromptu drum kit from saucepans, wooden spoons and whisks, Aki wanted to sing.

Next morning we drove with Igawa-san down to Tachibana. The crane hoisted the Slow Box from the truck and lowered the huge camera into the school car park. Just as it touched the ground we noticed something in the distance: a huge procession of children walking straight towards us across the paddy fields. It was a beautiful sight, but a little overwhelming. The musical ensemble sat down next to the camera and warmed up. The children got ever closer and soon enough had filled the car park. We looked out at hundreds of small Japanese eyes looking back at us expectantly, and so the band began to play and musical statues began. The children didn't really get it, I think they were a bit too sophisticated for such a primitive game. So we quit playing and tried to get them to sit down in an orderly way while Koi emphasised the importance of being still. Eventually Shin was ready and the exposure began. Of course the children moved, twitched and generally fidgeted for 10 minutes. When Shin eventually emerged from the Slow Box, there was a huge sigh of relief.

Takizawa Village, 15 July 2003 (left and right)

Kurokara Village, 20 July 2003 (left and right)

Tachibana community, 2 August 2003 (left and right)

After Image installation in the school gym at Kurokura Village, 7-31August 2000. Twenty-seven plates were arranged according to the sequence of the Slow Box's journey through Tsumari the previous month.

Takakura Village, 12 July 2003 (landscape-format camera)

Portraits of a brother and sister at Takakura Village, 13 July 2003 (suitcase camera)

Kurokura Village, 22 July 2003 (suitcase camera)

Kurokura Village, 23 July 2003 (suitcase camera)

Portrait of a couple at Kurokura Village, 23 July 2003 (suitcase camera)

Portrait of a couple at Takakura Village, 12 July 2003 (suitcase camera)

Takizawa Village, 16 July 2000 (Slow Box)

Funasaka Village, 28 July 2000 (Slow Box)

Kurokura Village, 21 July 2000 (Slow Box)

Kettou Village, 23 July 2000 (Slow Box)

Takakura Village, July 2000 (Slow Box)

House in Funasaka, July 2000 (Slow Box)

Grass-cutting day, Koshirakura, August 2003

Snow, Songline and Infrastructure (Network)

The flight from London passes right over Niigata, less than half an hour before we land at Narita airport. Then we spend more than four hours travelling overland to get back to the region where Koshirakura village is located. One hour to Tokyo Central via the Narita Express, then two-and-a-half hours to Echigo Yuzawa station by the bullet train, then one hour on the local two-carriage train on the Hokuhoku line, to arrive at Toukamachi station on the east side of Shinano River. Kawanishi is on the west side, and has only a bus link. In front of the small tobacco shop at Toukamachi station, we find a timetable painted on a metal plate: buses to Koshirakura 12.45 and 5.45. This twice-a-day connection began in 1997; a government subsidy makes up for the lack of regular commuters.

The bus ride takes a good hour as it goes from village to village, following the meandering course of the narrow Shibumi River. The road is made up of a patchwork of new and old, narrow and wide, smooth asphalt and concrete slabs, with grass growing in the cracks between them. Koshirakura's shrine is estimated to date back to at least the late seventeenth century. Some historians maintain that this community descends from Samurai warriors who took refuge in remote mountain areas after they lost a battle. They hid themselves, keeping their swords ready for the future, while temporarily living as farmers. This is the story most locals wish to believe.

Some archaeologists argue that the history of inhabitation stretches back much further, pointing to the fact that this area of Niigata was the capital of mainland Japan in the prehistoric Jyomon Period. People then survived through hunting, gathering and loosely organised rice cultivation. In this respect the local environment was ideal. When the snow fell in winter it covered the mountains with a hard surface of ice that smoothed out the topography. Journeys were quicker as it was easy to travel over the compacted snow. The cold climate was also ideal for preserving vegetables and fish. People used a communal 'fridge' – a hole in the ground with steps built down into it. Inside, there was a frame structure forming a small room where sake, vegetables and fish could be stored in a pile of packed snow. The snow would be covered with very thick layers of straw as insulation to preserve it all year round.

Besides food and materials, stories and a song travelled across this icy landscape.

Songs Along the Landscape

Different versions of the local song, 'Tenjinbayashi', are found across the region. They have been passed from generation to generation and from village to village across the mountains. The songline runs along the alpine ridges and through the river valleys, developing differently along each route.

The songline extends all the way to Tohoku in the far north of Japan, a place that bears no resemblance to Koshirakura, even if their songs are similar.

'Emu, Sanjeev and an Old Woman in Red' 6 September 1997

The old woman was sitting on a chair in front of her house. She had been dressed by her family in a bright-red traditional costume, so creating her very own 88-year-old ceremony.

Her small face beneath the big red hat seemed puzzled, but there was more than enough reason for this. Right in front of her was Sanjeev, beating Indian drums to a very different rhythm from any she knew.

Sanjeev towered over her, and the young people around her were singing and clapping their hands in time with the rhythm. Jumping up and down and dancing in a circle around her with both hands waving above his head was Emu, from Tokyo.

Who are these people? Sanjeev's only association with architecture was his friend Nimit, then a student at the AA. Emu, too, knew little about architecture, but had come here to think about his further education in design.

'Before Object, After Image' installation in AA Gallery, October 2006.

Sanjeev and Emu themselves had enough reason to be confused during the workshop. Their companions were spending a lot of time measuring things and drawing on sheets of paper, making various kinds of objects with different materials. Seven days before the festival, the whole team began practising Koshirakura's traditional song, 'Tenjinbayashi'. Sanjeev is a professional drummer, so it was very natural for him to adapt this rather non-rhythmic line of song into his own tune, with the help of Emu, who recorded the song and played it back and forward to analyse it.

The festival is normally carried out in stages. Making the decorations for the shrine takes seven evenings. On the eve of the festival a ritual takes place on the mountain to find the designated god-tree (a maple). The tree is cut in the early morning and carried down the mountain to the shrine, allowing the god to stay and wait for the festival to begin the next day. And then the maple tree is dragged round the village, bringing the god to each house to celebrate the good fortune of the families.

By the time the tree arrived in front of the old woman in red, Sanjeev had already played 'Tenjinbayashi' at least ten times.

Each time it was sung the song was transformed, little by little, from the original to the Sanjeev version.

Tenjinbayashino umenohana
Hitoedaoritewa kasanisasu
Kasanisasuyorimo shimazakino
Jyorouno teniageyo
Medetaimononiwa daikodane
Hanagasaitekara miganareba
Tawarakasanaru

Sanjeev knelt down in front of the old woman and kissed her feet according to Indian custom, and then Emu followed. The old woman whispered something to her daughter, her expression emerging from the many wrinkles of her small face. Her daughter explained, 'She says she thought she was in heaven already, with this group of young people around her... It was worth waiting this long, because now the world has come to see her.'

Another old woman said: 'I'm next', and a guy said, 'No, it's my turn now, SANJI-BU.'

We all know that standard units of measurement cannot adequately describe distance in our modern world. Networks of transport and communication often have a greater impact than distance in defining a locality, its economy and therefore the density of its population. But this size of population doesn't count the number of people flying overhead. It doesn't include the number of people who can sing 'Tenjinbayashi'.

Koshirakura has been excluded from the post-agricultural development of Japan during the late twentieth century. Ninety per cent of the population (the majority of whom are over 60) has never had any close encounter with foreigners. In a sense, inviting a group of AA students to occupy a former school building at the heart of the village was perhaps the most radical vision that the local government could have. Yet the chemistry of this intervention seemed to work. In 2005, the village decided to continue the workshop even after the dissolution of the Kawanishi government.

The slow 10 years of the first phase is to be followed by a second phase of 20 years (the life-cycle of structures made from maple wood). This lengthy process balances the temporal and the permanent, the international and the vernacular, reality and imagination.

Over 10 years the workshop has evolved as a very loose organisation. It has no office, no address, no contact phone; it exists purely as united informal networks between people. It becomes visible only once a year in August.

It can shrink and expand. If the entire workshop could be seen as a model, it would be a working model of recursion.

Despite our original agenda, we have learned over the years that there is no point in addressing questions of why people leave the place – or conversely why they might stay. Making objects became a means of communication, as well as a model for documenting architecture as a form of life-expression.

The workshop visualises and demonstrates invisible connections over varying distances. As a result, it is a live project of the landscape. We illuminate the role of an architect, abandoning the notion of office/studio and trying to relate distance and scale and time-span to people and a sense of place.

It is the model of something too big to see at once, longer and larger than the life of architecture and the architect that we may refer to as landscape.

Perhaps what we have enjoyed documenting is the natural recurrence of a series of extreme contrasts: the rural and the international, the young and the old, long periods and brief moments, events and buildings, function and fun, intelligence and craziness – all the things that cannot be measured using conventional sizes or scales.

There is a sense of beauty in the picture of a bright white satellite dish attached to the mud wall of a thatched house where an 88-year-old woman in red meets Sanjeev and Emu and an aeroplane flies in the sky above them.

The scale is between the enormity of the landscape and the smallness of a person.

The speed is between the speed of aeroplane and that of tree growth – something that 'Tenjinbayashi' and the satellite dish combine to transmit.

The timescale lies between every hour, every week and the period of 10 years.

The system is small and big, short and continuous, young and old, local and international.

A bus shelter, summer and winter pavilions, platforms, cinema props and screen, a singing stage, a gigantic camera, portable shrines with a big mouth and a swing-trap... were constructed with the help of:

80 or more laptops, websites, traditional tools, timber, clay, sandstone boulders, local songs, sake, snow, water, rope and a big screen to project visions as large as we wanted from a distance as far as we could remember.

In a total of 36 weeks divided over a period of 10 years:
200 architectural students, made up of 40 different nationalities, have stayed in the village over the summer
The ceremonial maple tree has increased in size (to twice its former diameter)
4 houses have gone
18 small buildings have been constructed
3 major earthquakes have flattened 3 of them
3 films were made
the Town Hall closed
we won 3 costume contests in the regional parade
There have been 10 festivals
10 cycles of grass-cutting
lots of singing and drinking
many karaoke sessions
32 firework displays
3 marriages
4 babies
one website

The population is 75.
There are 25 houses
and more diaries.

During the last 10 years Koshirakura Village has shrunk in size and grown in scale. It's louder in summer and still quiet in winter.

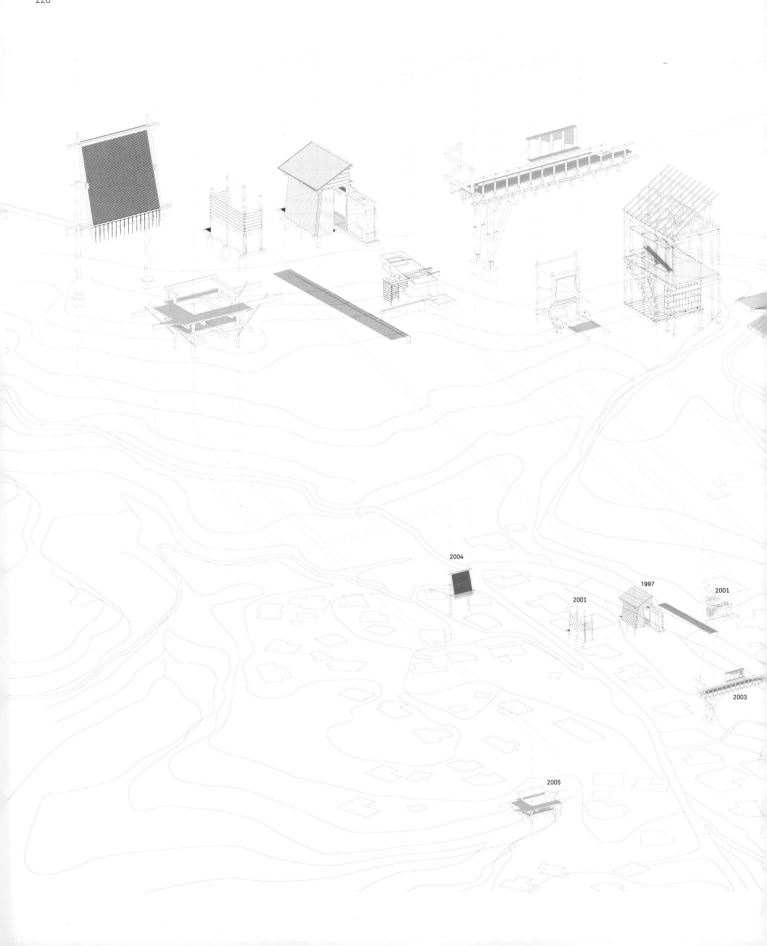

2004

2001

1997

2001

2003

2005

1998

1998-1999

2002

2001-2002

1999

1999

2001

2005

2005